T0119780

How to Live,
What to Do

MUSE BOOKS

The Iowa Series in Creativity and Writing

Robert D. Richardson, series editor

How

THIRTEEN WAYS

to Live,

OF LOOKING AT

What

WALLACE STEVENS

to Do

JOAN RICHARDSON

UNIVERSITY OF IOWA PRESS, Iowa City

University of Iowa Press, Iowa City 52242
Copyright © 2018 by the University of Iowa Press
www.uipress.uiowa.edu
Printed in the United States of America

Design by Richard Hendel

The University of Iowa Press is a member of Green Press Initiative
and is committed to preserving natural resources.

Printed on acid-free paper

Library of Congress Cataloging-in-Publication Data
Names: Richardson, Joan, 1946– author.
Title: How to live, what to do : thirteen ways of looking at Wallace
Stevens / Joan Richardson.
Description: Iowa City : University Of Iowa Press, [2018] |
Series: Muse books | Includes bibliographical references and index.
Identifiers: LCCN 2017039377 (print) | LCCN 2017050860 (ebk) |
ISBN 978-1-60938-550-7 (ebk) | ISBN 978-1-60938-549-1
(pbk : acid-free paper)
Subjects: LCSH: Stevens, Wallace, 1879–1955—Criticism and
interpretation. | BISAC: LITERARY CRITICISM / Poetry. |
BIOGRAPHY & AUTOBIOGRAPHY / Literary.
Classification: LCC PS3537.T4753 (ebk) |
LCC PS3537.T4753 Z7579 2018 (print) | DDC 811/.54—dc23
LC record available at https://lccn.loc.gov/2017039377

To the memory of ROBERTO PICCIOTTO
&
for my teachers and students

The river is moving.

The blackbird must be flying.

CONTENTS

My involvement with Wallace Stevens and his work began a long time ago, in a high school infatuation with his anthologized poems; it continued through my undergraduate years, when I hoped that my training in philosophy (my major) might help me penetrate his complexly beautiful surfaces to reach meanings, to get to the *true subjects* of his poems. My doggedness persisted: in graduate school I first pursued the history of metaphor, beginning with the pre-Socratics and ending with the symbolist poets, before going on—properly prepared, I thought—to complete a dissertation on Stevens. But still the greater number of his poems remained opaque. I then spent the next ten years or so reading everything I knew Stevens had read as I imagined him moving through the cycles of his life, from his childhood in Reading, Pennsylvania, through his maturity, aging, and death in Hartford, Connecticut. The constant in this passage was his attention to light.

In composing the two-volume critical biography that is the record of what I learned through those years, I attempted to make my sensibility his as much as possible, even for a while cultivating the habit of drinking martinis, Stevens's preferred beverage at lunch; the waitress at the Canoe Club in Hartford even knew that Stevens's order of a martini meant a pitcher. I restricted myself to cocktail hour and one martini glass—after all, Stevens was a tall

and portly man. In any case, I did not realize how success-
fully I had mimicked my subject until I set down—with
fountain pen on foolscap—the last words of my biography's final chapter, "the poet's bond to all that dust," and
then looked out the window at the leaves trembling in the
light summer air to find myself almost completely undone
as I recognized that after so many years I was seeing the
leaves with my own eyes again. At that moment I knew
I would never undertake another biography. Yet the rela-
tionships I developed with some of the "studious ghosts"
I came to know through tracking Stevens have become as
intimate as, if not more intimate than, the relationship I
continue to enjoy with him as interior paramour. This is
especially the case with William James, whom I currently
characterize playfully to my students as "my best imagi-
nary friend," although for a long time the designation belonged to Ralph Waldo Emerson. And my involvements
with Jonathan Edwards and Charles Sanders Peirce also
continue to deepen. In the truest sense, Wallace Stevens
has educated and continues to educate me.

When Bob Richardson—there is no family connection,
as far as we know—asked me to consider writing a volume
on Stevens for the Muse Books series, I resisted. I did not
want to immerse myself in Stevens again—particularly because a long-range creative project of my own was beck-
oning for full attention, but also because I could not
immediately imagine how I could offer, within a twenty-
five-thousand word limit, everything a reader new to
Stevens would need to know in order to move easily in his
"fluent mundo." But if I resisted undertaking the project, I
found it impossible to resist Bob, whose intellectual contributions and companionship over the decades—despite the
fact that we have been in each other's actual presence on
only one occasion—have provided me with essential nourishment. It was out of my deep appreciation of and grati-

[*About the Book*]

tude to him that I acceded to his request and put together a proposal for *How to Live, What to Do*. It was only after pondering for a good while how to do what I proposed that I devised its form, and so was added the subtitle, *Thirteen Ways of Looking at Wallace Stevens*.

Once I embarked on the project, the thirteen headings presented themselves with unexpected insistence, as though from some deep well within me. I thought of my task as somewhat similar to that set for himself by one of Stevens's favorite contemporary philosophers, who under the pen name Alain (Emile Chartier, 1868–1951) published regular columns in a provincial French newspaper in which he dealt with significant philosophical subjects but in language accessible to a nonprofessional, nonspecialist audience. Alain allowed himself eleven hundred words for each column, composed without erasures or cross-outs. While I did not impose on myself the same severe discipline, keeping roughly within a two-thousand word limit for each of the thirteen ways changed the nature of my relationship with thinking and writing: word count, as any good journalist or practitioner of haiku knows, demands that every word must indeed count. Forging each sentence against the constraint of concision—a primary virtue for Henry James, although on the surface one would be hard put to see his novels as evidence—forces an acute attention to and distillation of thinking, the measure of which is an inverse relationship between time and space: the time spent in composing and the space on the page. This kind of exercise turns out to be the ideal corrective to life in our moment, when for most of us it seems as if there is no time left to think. In our accelerated climate we do gradually but actually lose the sense of thinking, how it *feels*. It was most appropriate to Stevens that this project imposed its limit, since it is, finally, thinking that was his subject. Without the enforced verbal economy, I would not have become so keenly sensitive to the difficult wonder that thinking is, coming to experience fully the fact informing Jonathan Edwards's piercing observation, "The mind feels when it thinks."

Within the economy of this volume readers might at first be surprised to find certain repetitions. They are deliberate, reflecting a manner of recursive amplification that characterizes not only Stevens's style but also the actuality of my witnessing, attending to, and recording the process of thinking that this text represents. What I am referring to here will become clear as readers move through the thirteen ways. I have also intentionally not indicated page numbers for the quoted phrases and lines from Stevens's poems embedded in my text, for two reasons. First, these fragments arise as they do because they have become part of my language; one could fairly say that I have learned to speak Stevens. I did not, in thinking, go searching for these locutions; they are essential elements of my thinking. Second, when readers do not recognize the poem from which the words are taken but find themselves *called* by a particular line or phrase, I want to encourage them to go to the online Stevens concordance and begin exploring the territory of his being by locating the setting of the words in the poem from which they came. In this way each reader will, I hope, come to inhabit certain of Stevens's rooms of ideas, begin to feel at home in this stanza or that, and return to rest and *muse in* it periodically. In contrast, I have indicated page numbers for passages of any length from Stevens's prose, notebooks, and letters, since the concordance does not yet have this material in its fund. Here and there I have taken verbal liberties in the spirit of Stevens that I trust readers will appreciate.

ABBREVIATIONS

The titles of the following works have been abbreviated for convenience. Quotations from them in the text and references in the notes are identified by abbreviated title and page number.

CPP   Wallace Stevens. *Collected Poetry and Prose.*
        Edited by Frank Kermode and Joan Richardson.
        New York: Library of America, 1997.
L   Holly Stevens, ed. *Letters of Wallace Stevens.*
        New York: Alfred A. Knopf, 1966.

How to Live, What to Do

I

Wallace Stevens was born in 1879, a time in America, and in the West generally, when the religion in which one was reared provided guidance about how to live, what to do. Between that moment and his death in 1955, the world changed dramatically—Stevens's life span was exactly the same as Albert Einstein's, and he came into his maturity as a poet in the years just after Einstein's discoveries. Throughout the first half of the twentieth century, as the dust from the explosion of Charles Darwin's discoveries began to settle, disruptions in addition to Einstein's revelations disturbed both our sense of what it is to be human and our understanding of the nature of physical reality. Everything, in Stevens's words, was set "hissing and spinning." He described it as follows to those gathered at the University of Chicago on November 16, 1951, to hear his Moody Lecture, "A Collect of Philosophy":

> The material world, for all the assurances of the eye, has become immaterial. It has become an image in the mind. The solid earth disappears and the whole atmosphere is subtilized not by the arrival of some venerable beam of light from an almost hypothetical star but by a breach of reality. What we see is not an external world but an image of it and hence an internal world. (*CPP* 857)

A few months earlier, in April, he had delivered another lecture, titled simply "Two or Three Ideas," to the members of the College English Association at its annual meeting at Mount Holyoke College in South Hadley, Massachusetts. He offered a moving description of the condition in which the creatures of our culture found themselves in the wake of the wonderful but terrifying discoveries of the modern world:

> To see the gods dispelled in mid-air and dissolve like clouds is one of the great human experiences. It is not as if they had gone over the horizon to disappear for a time; nor as if they had been overcome by other gods of greater power and profounder knowledge. It is simply that they came to nothing. Since we have always shared all things with them and have always had a part of their strength and, certainly, all of their knowledge, we shared likewise this experience of annihilation. It was their annihilation, not ours, and yet it left us feeling that in a measure we, too, had been annihilated. It left us feeling dispossessed and alone in a solitude, like children without parents, in a home that seemed deserted, in which the amical rooms and halls had taken on a look of hardness and emptiness. What was most extraordinary is that they left no mementoes behind, no thrones, no mystic rings, no texts either of the soil or of the soul. It was as if they had never inhabited the earth. There was no crying out for their return. They were not forgotten because they had been a part of the glory of the earth. At the same time, no man ever muttered a petition in his heart for the restoration of those unreal shapes. There was always in every man the increasingly human self, which instead of remaining the observer, the non-participant, the delinquent,

became constantly more and more all there was or so it seemed; and whether it was so or merely seemed so still left it for him to resolve life and the world in his own terms.

Stevens then specified the subject of his address: "To speak of the origin and the end of gods is not a light matter. It is to speak of the origin and end of eras of human belief.... In an age of disbelief ... it is for the poet to supply the satisfactions of belief, in his manner and in his style.... It is," he announced, "a spiritual role" (*CPP* 842).

Throughout his career Stevens would offer "notations of the wild, the ruinous waste," but would consistently underscore the salvific power of the imagination in the face of the actual: "the violence from within that protects us from the violence without." In a late letter to a friend about the years he spent at Harvard (as a special student from 1897 to 1900), he commented that what William James had called the "will to believe" in the face of the ever increasing "wild facts"—another of James's phrasings—hung over everything.[1] Knowing that will in himself, Stevens created his "fluent mundo," in which all of us who are his readers come to experience at least "momentary existence on an exquisite plane."

As Stevens stated so clearly, in such an uncertain time— extending even more tensively into our own—it is the role of the poet to offer guidance about "how to live, what to do" (the title of a poem from *Ideas of Order*, 1936), a function that had been provided for earlier generations by the Bible and its ministers. Stevens took on this responsibility. In doing so he was following examples he himself had learned from and valued. Significantly, one set of models was drawn from the West, and the other from the East.

From the West, Stevens was deeply indebted to the British and other European romantic and later symbolist poets, all of whom prized inner vision in its intimate relation with nature. He was intent on having his corpus, *Collected Poems*, serve as a secular bible, a "world-book" in the manner of Novalis and of Friedrich Schlegel, who wrote, "For my own part, the goal of my literary projects is to write a new Bible," to explicate nature and human beings' place in it.[2] This aspiration was shared by Ralph Waldo Emerson, whose work Stevens began reading early in his life. His mother presented the young poet with the twelve-volume Houghton edition (1896–1898) of Emerson's *Works* for Christmas in 1898; Stevens marked many of the essays and incorporated innumerable phrases and references from Emerson into his own poetic vocabulary. (These volumes, which the poet kept throughout his life, now belong to the Wallace Stevens Collection at the Huntington Library in San Marino, California.) In concluding the final essay of *Representative Men* (1850), "Goethe; or, The Writer," Emerson exhorted, "We too must write Bibles, to unite again the heavens and the earthly world." Stevens took this incitement to heart and mind.

It was Emerson as well who first opened for Stevens the doors to the East, not only to the ancient *Sacred Books of The East*, a fifty-volume set of English translations of Asian religious writings filled with hymns to nature, but also to their dissemination in later forms through Buddhism. "The Buddhist," Emerson observed, "is a Transcendentalist." At the close of his Divinity School Address (delivered to the graduating class of Harvard Divinity School in 1838), Emerson enjoined the following:

> I look for the new Teacher, that shall follow so far those shining laws, that he shall see them come full circle; shall see their rounding complete grace; shall see the world to be the mirror of the soul; shall see the identity of the law of gravitation with purity of

heart; and shall show that the Ought, that Duty, is one thing with Science, with Beauty, and with Joy.[3]

Stevens answered this call.

Incorporating the idea of the "world-book" and Stéphane Mallarmé's later iteration in the form of "*le Grand Oeuvre*" (the Great, or Grand, Work), Stevens wanted to title his own final collection "The Whole of Harmonium: The Grand Poem." (To the poet's regret, his publisher, Alfred Knopf, persuaded him that the simpler, more direct *Collected Poems* made better marketing sense.) In selecting the poems for this last and lasting volume, Stevens remembered another lesson he had learned along the way from the East. There was keen interest in all things Asian at Harvard during Stevens's time as a student: there had been the opening of Japan to the West in midcentury; the current news of the Boxer Rebellion in China; Ernest Fenollosa's contributions to the Oriental Collection of the Boston Museum of Fine Arts; and increasing scholarly work branching from F. Max Müller's translations of Sanskrit texts and Japanese Buddhist tracts. (Later in his life Stevens referred to Müller as the foremost Orientalist of his day—before the term became politically incorrect—and indicated that he shared the excitement about his work, as Emerson had earlier.) Also among Stevens's cohort while an undergraduate were Arthur Davison Fiske and Witter Bynner; the three were immersed in discovering as much as they could about the art and literature of China and Japan, and Stevens developed an enduring friendship with Bynner. Pursuing this interest, Bynner eventually made two extended visits to the East: to Japan and China in 1917, and to China again for almost a year in 1921. During the 1920s Bynner collaborated on translations of Lao-tzu and of a major Chinese anthology; the latter was published in 1929 under the title *The Jade Moun-*

*tain: A Chinese Anthology (Being Three Hundred Poems of
the T'ang Dynasty, 618–906).*

As Stevens shaped his personal anthology, the volume
that would "take the place of a mountain"—an integral
part of the "intelligence of his soil"—he recalled what he
had read years earlier concerning what the "old Chinese"
considered the perfect anthology. From Bynner and Kiang
Kang-Hu's introduction to *The Jade Mountain*, he learned
that the Chinese believed that approximately three hundred poems constitute the ideal number for an anthology.
This was based on the old saying that "By reading thoroughly three hundred T'ang poems, one will write verse
without learning."[4] Such a volume was an integral part
of any Chinese household—like the Bible in traditional
American homes—and was to be read from every day in
an ongoing attempt to harmonize human experience with
the tremors and constantly demanding changes of nature.
The perfect Chinese anthology was thought of as a secular sacred book. To those family members who could not
read, the poems were read aloud. Stevens's memories of
his mother's voice intoning phrases of Bible stories while
he and his siblings prepared for bed—it was her habit to
read a chapter from the Bible to them every night—mixed
with his recollection of this bit of Chinese cultural history.
His *Collected Poems* number 301. (It should be noted, too,
that for the Chinese the preferred total number was to be
odd: 301, 305, or 311, for instance.)

By thoroughly reading Stevens's 301 poems through
the cycle of the seasons, year after year, one can come to
write verse without learning: his *Collected Poems* is a script
for a human, not a divine, comedy. His project, "the cosmic poem of the ascent into heaven" (*CPP* 859), was to include all he could understand in his lifetime, not only from
his direct contact with nature but also from what he read
about developments in science and the philosophical tra-

ditions of West and East. Thinking about thinking as it responded to and traced through history our "bond to all that dust" in the "imperfect [that] is our paradise" would, he hoped, demonstrate "the identity of the law of gravitation with purity of heart."

2

The most formative and enduring of the experiences fram-
ing "the compass and curriculum" of Stevens's poetry
began, as it were, at his mother's knee, hearing her voice
carrying the cadences of the King James Bible as he prepared for bed and then lulling him into sleep. Later in his
life, while a student at Harvard and afterward making his
way in New York City, he often commented in his journal and in letters to Elsie Moll, his future wife, on his still
"hankering after hymns" even as his faith diminished:
"The feeling of piety is very dear to me. I would sacrifice a
great deal to be a Saint Augustine but modernity is so Chicagoan, so plain, so unmeditative"; "I wish that groves still
were sacred—or, at least, that something was. . . . I grow
tired of the want of faith—the instinct of faith" (*L* 32, 86).
He was particularly involved with Psalms, as evidenced
by his markings in the copy of the Bible he kept into his
maturity (also part of the Wallace Stevens Collection at the
Huntington Library). Of the 73 (of a total of 150) psalms
attributed to King David, 13 relate specifically to incidents
in the king's life, and in the King James translation his
prayer is called a cry. "The poem is the cry of its occasion, /
Part of the res itself and not about it," Stevens offers in "An
Ordinary Evening in New Haven."

Between the pages of his Bible, in Psalms, Stevens laid

a newspaper clipping (undated) that suggests how to read the thirty-one chapters of Proverbs, the book that follows Psalms: read one a day, and "at the end of the month you will be surprised to find how many problems of right and wrong have been solved for you."[1] There is no evidence that Stevens practiced this exercise, but he seems to have adapted the suggestion to fashion his own breviary drawn from the Psalms. He circled the numbers of verses in many, underlined certain other verses, and in some cases indicated entire psalms, adding circlings, checkmarks, and underlinings. He quoted from Psalm 19 to Elsie in a letter: "Day unto day uttereth speech, and night unto night sheweth knowledge." Above Psalm 100, "A Psalm of Praise," Stevens wrote, "An exhortation to praise God cheerfully."

That the letter *C* is the roman numeral for the arabic number 100 seems, given Stevens's notation, to be one of the hints surrounding the naming of "The Comedian as the Letter C." On the inside back cover of one of his notebooks—the last entry, dated January 10, 1901—Stevens copied verse 19 from the gimel section of Psalm 119: "I *am* a stranger in the earth: hide not thy commandments from me." Gimel is the third letter of the Hebrew alphabet, equivalent to the English *G* but corresponding in Latin to both *C* and *G*; it is used as a subheading in the King James translation of Psalm 119 as a reminder that each of the verses in this section—a stanza in Hebrew—begins with the letter gimel. There are twenty-two stanzas in this psalm, an alphabetical acrostic in which each stanza consists of eight lines all beginning with the same Hebrew letter; the twenty-two stanzas use all twenty-two letters of the Hebrew alphabet sequentially in an extended paean to God's law. The elaborate play on and with the sounds of letters and words was not lost on the poet in his later persona as "The Comedian." Stevens would also have known that the Greek root of the word "psalm," *psallo*, is a verb meaning "to pluck, to play a stringed instrument"; his "Man with the Blue Guitar" is an avatar of David.

Concentrated, intense attention characterizes prayer in all its forms, from voicing desolation and calling for solace to expanding the spirit into a sacrament of praise for mere being—as Emerson offered in *Nature* (1836), "Is not prayer also ... a sally of the soul into the unfound infinite?"[2] Throughout his career as a poet, Stevens stretched his early expressed wish that something remain sacred into a habit of mind that uncovered the miraculous in the ordinary or, perhaps better, revealed the ordinary to be miraculous—in this again recalling a lesson learned from Emerson: "The invariable mark of wisdom is to see the miraculous in the common."[3] In "quiz[zing] all sounds, all thoughts, all everything," in what he called the "exquisite environment of fact," including the fact of his own thinking, Stevens also affiliated himself with an earlier priest of the invisible whose spirit continued to inhabit the Connecticut Valley: Jonathan Edwards. Edwards described God as "a communicating being" whose disclosures are revealed to us through our giving close "attention of the mind in thinking." This exercise was, for Edwards, the purest form of piety, requiring what he described as "being's consent to Being," an activity demanding repeated renewal, the persistent turning and returning of attention to an aspect of creation until it yielded the secret of its place and purpose. *Consent*, for Edwards, carried its full etymological weight as "feeling with"—feeling with what he described as the "sense of the heart," an additional sense to our usual five, activated by recognizing what he particularized as the "excitement" pulsating in our various responses to this or that "part or particle of God," in Emerson's later phrasing.[4]

It is in this kind of engagement that we and the world around us come to tremble in transparencies of recognition. Drawing on Luce Irigaray's observations concerning the integral connection between breathing and forms of prayer, a scholar of the phenomenology of prayer has noted that "there is an infinity of … modalities" of feeling in experience, "changes in the time, texture, space, and rest, or articulation of silence, sound, and movement that are constantly changing in relation to the external and internal environments of the psyche and soma."[5] Stevens came to excel in closely attending to and scoring his arc of being within this infinity.

While still a young man, he observed in his journal, "I'm completely satisfied that behind every physical fact there is a divine force. Don't, therefore, look at facts, but through them" (*L* 32). He recorded this entry in August 1899, not long after receiving his mother's Christmas gift of the Emerson volumes. There, in the first volume, he read Emerson's 1841 oration, "The Method of Nature"—a provocative title for someone like Stevens, so attuned from childhood to the beauty of the natural world—where he would have read that

> man … must look at nature with a supernatural eye. By piety alone, by conversing with the causes of nature, is he safe and commands it. And because all knowledge is assimilation to the object of knowledge, as the power or genius of nature is ecstatic, so must its science or the description of it be. The poet must be a rhapsodist: his inspiration a sort of bright casualty; his will in it only the surrender of will to the Universal Power, which will not be seen face to face, but must be received and sympathetically known.[6]

And in the third volume Stevens would have found this stirring description in the first essay, "The Poet":

> As the eyes of Lyncaeus were said to see through the earth, so the poet turns the world to glass, and shows

us all things in their right series and procession. For, through that better perception, he stands one step nearer to things, and sees the flowing or metamorphosis; perceives that thought is multiform; that within the form of every creature is a force impelling it to ascend to a higher form; and following with his eyes the life, uses the forms which express that life, and so his speech flows with the flowing of nature.[7]

Stevens became an "inquisitive botanist" early in life, assiduously setting down in his notebooks and journals the details of his conversations with nature gathered from the "bright casualty" of what caught or held his attention on the extended walks that were the experiential fabric onto which he stitched the intricate patterns of his perception into poems: snow, for example, became "like eyesight falling to earth." He took to heart what he learned from Emerson in the seminal "Language" chapter of *Nature*:

A man conversing in earnest, if he watch his intellectual processes, will find that a material image, more or less luminous, arises in his mind, cotemporaneous with every thought, which furnishes the vestment of the thought. Hence, good writing and brilliant discourse are perpetual allegories. This imagery is spontaneous. It is the blending of experience with the present action of the mind. It is proper creation. It is the working of the Original Cause through the instruments he has already made.[8]

Even before leaving Reading, Pennsylvania, for Harvard, Stevens realized (and commented on in his journal) the threat posed by increasing industrialization to being able to cultivate the "habits of conversation with nature" urged by Emerson in "History."[9] The once limpid air in the countryside around Reading had already begun to be polluted by smoke belching from factory chimneys. The American pastoral rhythm of life, with farmers and their families rising with the light and ending their activities as night fell, was being transformed by the laying of additional rail lines and the imposition of standard time to make train scheduling possible. Stevens registered these "velocities of change" and attempted to preserve the Lucretian borders of his being by incorporating into his routine, insofar as the weather allowed, long walks into whatever preserves of nature were available in the various localities where he resided.

While he was still in Reading, and on visits back home on holidays after he had moved to Cambridge, Massachusetts, his walks took him into the fertile valleys and gentle woods of Berks, Bucks, and Lancaster Counties, where even today one sees the Amish tending their fields and moving along the still quiet roads in horse-drawn carriages. In Cambridge there was (and is) Mount Auburn Cemetery—the first large-scale designed landscape in the United States, with its tower and the surrounding countryside to the north introducing English landscape style to the "new world," creating a place where shepherds might be imagined tending their flocks.

Once he was settled in New York City, first trying his hand at journalism and later attending law school, Stevens left the city almost every Sunday and walked into the New Jersey countryside, sometimes covering up to forty miles by the time he returned to his apartment in the early evening. There he would set down in his journal the details of what he had seen and felt and then reflect on these perceptions, much in the manner of the "good Puritans" (*L* 9) from whom he had descended, who used their journals to examine their spirits for signs of election. Unlike them, however, the young poet increasingly felt the withering of faith, yet the residual typological habit of reading the

Book of Nature in search of divinity remained. His sense of divinity came to be understood as William James would describe in *The Varieties of Religious Experience*: "*the feelings, acts, and experiences of individual men in their solitude, so far as they apprehend themselves to stand in relation to whatever they may consider the divine.*"[10]

Stevens met Elsie Moll back home in Reading during the summer of 1904, after he had passed the bar exam and been admitted to the practice of law in early June. Once he returned to New York in September, his letters to her began to supplement and then largely supplant his journal keeping. "My letters to Elsie usurp the chronicles that, but for them, I should set down here," he noted (*L* 94). In the city he set up a partnership with a law school friend—a venture that failed—then worked for several law firms before finding secure employment in 1908 as a member of the legal staff in the New York branch office of the American Bonding Company of Baltimore. He moved to East Orange, New Jersey, for a while and then to Fordham Heights in the Bronx before returning to live in Manhattan.

His letters filled the seasons spent away from Elsie throughout the five years of their courtship. In the deepening disclosures of preferences and habits in their epistolary intimacy—he called the accumulating letters "The Book of Doubts and Fears"—he encouraged her to cultivate her own variety of religious experience, including churchgoing, but announced something seemingly quite different for himself:

> I was more interested than you may believe in what you said about religion. A. T.'s [Alice Tragle, a friend of Elsie's] opinions are quite elementary. I have never told you what I believe. There are so many things to think of. I don't *care* whether the churches are all alike or whether they're right or wrong. It is not im-

portant. The very fact that they take care of A. T.'s "stupid" people is an exquisite device. It is undoubtedly true that they do not "*influence*" any but the "stupid." But they are beautiful and full of comfort and moral help. One can get a thousand benefits from churches that one cannot get outside of them. They purify a man, they soften Life. *Please* don't listen to A. T., or, at least, don't argue with her. Don't *care* about the Truth. There are other things in Life besides the Truth upon which everybody of any experience agrees, while no two people agree about the Truth. I'd rather see you going to church than know you were as wise as Plato and [Ernst] Haeckel rolled in one; and I'd rather sing some old chestnut out of the hymn-book with you, surrounded by "stupid" people, than listen to all the wise men in the world. It has always been a particular desire of mine to have you join church; and I am very, very glad to know that you are now on the road.—I am not in the least religious.

He continued with an explanation of his own sense of spirituality:

The sun clears my spirit, if I may say that, and an occasional sight of the sea, and thinking of blue valleys, and the odor of the earth, and many things. Such things make a god of a man; but a chapel makes a man of him. Churches are human.—I say my prayers every night—not that I need them now, or that they are anything more than a habit, half-unconscious. (*L* 96)

The elements of what became Stevens's project of secularizing the visionary are all here, as he laid out for his future wife the terms in which he believed that "Poetry /

Exceeding music must take the place / Of empty heaven and its hymns." He wrote to her of these things again just over two years later (May 2, 1909), during one of the periods when he was rereading Psalms, and clarified his beliefs and aspirations even more. As usual, he wrote to her after having taken his Sabbath walk, just as earlier he had recorded his long Sunday walks in his journal. This letter reveals both the images and the theme that would later be composed into "Sunday Morning," the first formal announcement of his naturalization of faith. I have quoted substantially from the letter, which is five times as long, and have added italics to emphasize the disclosures that would inform and underpin his poetics as well as certain images in his poem:

Sunday Evening

My dearest:

. . . Today I have been roaming about town. In the morning I walked down-town—stopping once to watch three *flocks of pigeons circling* in the sky. I dropped into St. John's chapel an hour before the service and sat in the last pew and looked around. It happens that last night at the Library I read a life of Jesus and I was interested to see what symbols of that life appeared in the chapel. I think there were none at all excepting the gold cross on the altar. *When you compare that poverty with the wealth of symbols, of remembrances, that were created and revered in times past, you appreciate the change that has come over the church. The church should be more than a moral institution, if it is to have the influence that it should have.* The space, the gloom, the quiet mystify and entrance the spirit. But that is not enough.—And one turns from this chapel to those built by men who *felt the wonder* of the life and death of Jesus—temples full of sacred images, full of the air of love and holiness—tabernacles hallowed by worship that sprang from the noble depths of men familiar with Gethsemane, familiar with Jerusalem.—*I do not wonder that the church is so largely a relic. Its vitality depended on its association with Palestine*, so to speak.—I felt a peculiar emotion in reading about John the Baptist, Bethany, Galilee—and so on, because (the truth is) I had not thought about them much since my days at Sunday-school (when, of course, I didn't think of them at all). *It was like suddenly remembering something long forgotten, or else like suddenly seeing something new and strange in what had always been in my mind.*—Reading the life of Jesus, too, makes one distinguish the separate idea of God. Before to-day I do not think I have ever realized that God was distinct from Jesus. It enlarges the matter almost beyond comprehension. People doubt the existence of Jesus—at least they doubt incidents of his life, such as, say, the Ascension into Heaven after his death. *But I do not understand that they deny God. I think everyone admits that in some form or other.—The thought makes the world sweeter—even if God be no more than the mystery of Life.*—Well, after a bit, I left the chapel and walked over the Brooklyn Bridge. There was a high wind, so that I put my hat under my arm.

After taking the subway back into Manhattan and walking uptown and then downtown again, he noted to Elsie:

I dropped into a church for five minutes, merely to see it, you understand. *I am not pious. But churches are beautiful to see.*—And then I came home, observing great masses of white clouds, with an autumnal shape to them, floating through the windy sky. . . .

I wish I could spend the whole season out of doors, walking by day, reading and studying in the evenings. I feel a tremendous capacity for enjoying that kind of life … and I imagine that when I come home from the Library, thinking over some capital idea—a new name for the Milky Way, a new aspect of Life, an amusing story, a gorgeous line—I am as happy as I should be—or could be—anywhere. (L 139–41)

In the fullness of his career in 1940, as he contemplated the establishment of a Chair of Poetry at Harvard, Stevens noted the following in his draft of the proposal: "The major poetic idea in the world is and always has been the idea of God. One of the visible movements of the modern imagination is the movement away from the idea of God. The poetry that created the idea of God will either adapt it to our different intelligence, or create a substitute for it, or make it unnecessary. These alternatives probably mean the same thing" (*CPP* 806).

Stevens knew in his being the power of the sacred texts in which he, as one of the inhabitants of the West, had been schooled; these texts had nourished his imagination. Ludwig Wittgenstein, a close contemporary, attentive to the same strains in their time, observed, "A *picture* held us captive. And we could not get outside it, for it lay in our language, and language seemed to repeat it to us inexorably."[11] Stevens's habit of saying his prayers remained as a residual container of faith, but he gradually refilled the shapes of those sounds with new forms drawn from his experience in the naturalized spacetime of his extended moment. As he expressed very near the end of his life, on receiving the National Book Award in 1955, the "reality" of the poet of his time—and in ours—is "that he lives in the world of Darwin and not in the world of Plato" (*CPP* 878). "Poetry, then, is the only possible heaven" (*L* 360). Reading his poems, we learn the same habit of close attention, intense concentration, demanded by prayer; his body of work a breviary, a primer in practicing a "constant sacrament of praise" for mere being. As Harold Bloom, "moved almost to tears" by reading and rereading Stevens's poems, recently expressed, "From start to end, his work is a solar litany.... Stevens has helped me to live my life."[12]

3

ECHOLOCATION

In lecturing and writing about the particular resonance of
the sound of Stevens's words in relation to the work of contemporary poet Susan Howe, an aspect she herself writes
about and celebrates, I have used the concept of echolocation to characterize the manner in which words that matter in fact *become* matter: they actually lead us—in the way
sonar signals do among certain kinds of bats, whales, and
some other creatures—to find nourishment, one another,
and other elements necessary for survival. As Stevens expressed so movingly in closing "The Noble Rider and the
Sound of Words," originally delivered as a lecture at Princeton University in May 1941:

> The deepening need for words to express our
> thoughts and feelings which, we are sure, are all the
> truth that we shall ever experience, having no illu-
> sions, makes us listen to words when we hear them,
> loving them and feeling them, makes us search the
> sound of them, for a finality, a perfection, an unalter-
> able vibration, which it is only within the power of
> the acutest poet to give them. . . .
>
> It is not an artifice that the mind has added to
> human nature. The mind has added nothing to
> human nature. It is a violence from within that pro-
> tects us from a violence without. It is the imagination

pressing back against the pressure of reality. It seems, in the last analysis, to have something to do with our self-preservation; and that, no doubt, is why the expression of it, the sound of its words, helps us to live our lives. (*CPP* 662, 665)

Of course, all poets echo other poets to some extent, sometimes intentionally but more often accidentally, finding themselves in a rhythm, cadence, or phrase that only in or after their own composing reveals itself to belong to another's voicing. My own sensitivity to this aspect of the sound of words began under the tutelage of John Hollander, with whom I was fortunate enough to have studied and who directed my dissertation. His exquisite little book, *The Figure of Echo: A Mode of Allusion in Milton and After* (1984), encapsulates his abundantly rich elucidation and tracing of resonance through time as it is perceived and registered by makers, listeners, and readers of poetry in mappings of influence.

What I am pointing to under the term *echolocation*, however, is something different, not an academic or historical tracing; rather, my address is to the primary process of poets, readers, and listeners who, in turning toward certain phenomena of sound, find themselves to be inhabited by the "studious ghosts" who shaped those sounds. In other words, my concern is the phenomenology of poetic experience, the frisson charging the moments when one feels directly addressed by a poem, recognized "more truly and more strange" in an uncanny inhabitation. This is a secular variety of religious experience, not different from the recognition wished for by Orthodox Christian believers in their veneration of icons, an engagement in which they come to feel not that they are looking at an image of Christ, the Virgin, or one of the saints but that *this figure is looking at them.* In effect, "all mean egotism vanishes" in these instances of what William James called "pure experience," when the subject-object divide is breached and "the currents of the Universal Being circulate through": "Nothing that is not there and the nothing that is."[1] I have intentionally run together Emerson's and Stevens's voices here in an attempt to capture, however feebly, the actuality of the poetic process as Stevens certainly knew it. Indeed, a description of this process comes to us famously from Samuel Taylor Coleridge, another poet devoted to translating divinity: "The primary Imagination I hold to be the living Power and prime Agent of all human Perception, and as a repetition in the finite mind of the eternal act of creation in the infinite I AM."[2]

The manner of this process will be familiar to readers who have found a particular phrase repeating itself periodically in their mind's ear without at first understanding why this trace appears, but who, in following it to its source within the texture of the whole of which it is a part, find there, as if by miracle, the answer to a question they have been pondering or find that the occasion of the source poem expresses their own cry: "It is safe to sleep to a sound that time brings back." Following the trace, or the echo, back to its source and noting where and when it emerged spatializes and temporalizes the experience, revealing something about the embodied relation so that the relation itself becomes a lived texture in which self and other, subject and object, are collapsed, all mean egotism vanished in transparency. Being overtaken by this kind of experience is a form of telepathy: "far-feeling," from the Greek *tele* and *pathos*, as William James described, "thought-transference, or the phenomenon of the reception by the mind of an impression not traceable to any of the ordinarily recognized channels of sense."[3] This phenomenon is equivalent to Jonathan Edwards's "sense of the heart."

As Edwards spelled out in his notes to himself elaborating this sense, in order for it to be perceptible it must be contained in what he called a "room of the idea"—a stanza, as it were, a prosodic habitation in which its pulsing can be felt.[4] "It is," Stevens indicated, "only within the power of the acutest poet" to create these rooms to which we return for comfort and sustenance. "Poetry is like prayer in that it is most effective in solitude and in the times of solitude as, for example, in the earliest morning.... Poetry is a health. ... Poetry is a cure of the mind" (*CPP* 903, 913).

Indeed, only the acutest poets achieve such sacraments—their poems are nothing less than transubstantiations of spirit that in turn transfigure the reader, "the listener in the snow," into "nothing that is not there and the nothing that is." These are moments of illumination, of "critical opalescence," of being figuratively bathed in sweat at the instant of enlightenment—the snowman described in the Diamond Sutra.[5] A precondition for accomplishing such secular miracles—Western versions of satori—is, of course, having been so affected, having found oneself "Engaged in the most prolific narrative, / A sound producing the things that are spoken." In the third lecture (chapter) of *The Varieties of Religious Experience* (1902), "The Reality of the Unseen," William James describes the "cosmical *It*" that informs "the human ontological imagination": "It is as if there were in the human consciousness a *sense of reality, a feeling of objective presence, a perception* of what we may call '*something there*,' more deep and more general than any of the special and particular 'senses' by which the current psychology supposes existent realities to be originally revealed."[6] In the absence of the traditional forms of prayer and ritual that prepare the imagination to experience the reality of the unseen, it is up to the poets to prepare us through poems that demand the kind of intense attention that belongs to prayer. By reading Stevens we learn to pray. The poet's role, he observed, "is to help people to live their lives" (*CPP* 661). "After one has abandoned a belief in god, poetry is that essence which takes its place as life's redemption" (*CPP* 901).

4

THE EXQUISITE ENVIRONMENT OF FACT

The exquisite environment of fact. The final poem
will be the poem of fact in the language of fact. But it will
be the poem of fact not realized before.

Poetry has to be something more than a conception
of the mind. It has to be a revelation of nature. Conceptions
are artificial. Perceptions are essential.

—*CPP* 904

These excerpts are from *Adagia*, Stevens's collection of aphorisms, and should be read against the background of spacetime and the quantum universe—reality as it came to be described during his lifetime.[1] This reality is the nature he would attempt to reveal through his various poetic experiments, thought experiments that were not different in kind from Einstein's as the physicist pondered the shape of the cosmos and the relation of its coordinates. The invisible new world was the environment the two men inhabited and that we continue to inhabit, made "exquisite" in description by Stevens's probing and searching—*ex* plus *quaerere*, to seek; the word itself is an example, the only noncompound word beginning with "exq" in Webster's Second Dictionary, one of the poet's important sources, his "basic slate." "The habit of probing for an integration seems to be part of the general will to order" (*CPP* 862).

What is it or how is it *to be* in spacetime, knowing that we are simultaneously suspended in, bombarded by, and penetrated through by fields of energy we can never see or feel? (More than one cosmic ray passes through a human hand every second; one mile beneath the earth's surface a ray passes through every two months.) "Let be be finale of seem" was not, for Stevens, simply a gnomic opening into the closing couplet of what would become one of his most anthologized poems, but a direction as densely packed with the particulars of what had been uncovered about our universe by the year he published his first volume as the atom, revealed to be not at all atomic but packed with particles ever smaller, more strange and charming, moving up and down, top to bottom ceaselessly. Reality indeed became the activity of the most august, most capable imagination. In "A Collect of Philosophy" Stevens observed that Max Planck ushered in a "century of intense thought" with his October 1900 discovery of quanta.[2] Stevens referred to Planck as "the patriarch of all modern physicists": he was "a much truer symbol of ourselves" than others because of his realization of "the provisional and changing creation of the power of the imagination," "his willingness to believe beyond belief" (*CPP* 866–87). Stevens quoted from a letter sent to him by Jean Paulhan, the coeditor (with the poet's friend Henry Church) of the little French magazine, *Mesures*, and the publisher and director of *La Nouvelle Revue Française* (which the poet regularly read). Stevens admired Paulhan as a "scholar . . . with an extremely aggressive mind" (*L* 376) and queried him about inherently poetic philosophical and/or scientific ideas. Paulhan responded to Stevens's letter (in French, the translation is Stevens's) as follows:

It is admitted, since Planck, that determinism—the relation of cause to effect—exists, or so it seems, on the human scale, only by means of an aggregate of statistical compensations and as the physicists say, by virtue of macroscopic approximations. (There is much to dream about in these macroscopic approximations.) As to the true nature of corpuscular or quantic phenomena, well, try to imagine them. No one has yet succeeded. But the poets—it is possible....

It comes to this that philosophers (particularly the philosophers of science) make not discoveries but hypotheses that may be called poetic. Thus Louis de Broglie admits that progress in physics is, at the moment, in suspense because we do not have the words or the images that are essential to us. But to create illuminations, images, words, that is the very reason for being of poets. (*CPP* 861)

To give an accurate sense of the perceptual field underpinning the quantum reality of the modernist moment, Stevens offered the following description from Alfred North Whitehead's *Science and the Modern World*—a seminal text for the twentieth and twenty-first centuries: "My theory involves the entire abandonment of the notion that simple location is the primary way in which things are involved in spacetime. In a certain sense, everything is everywhere at all times. For every location involves an aspect of itself in every other location. Thus every spatio-temporal standpoint mirrors the world." Stevens then offered a vivid précis of his aesthetic as a response to this monumental shift in conceptualizing our cosmic situation, the conceptualizing itself being a form of "cosmic poetry": "These words are pretty obviously words from a level where every-

thing is poetic, as if the statement that every location involves an aspect of itself in every other location produced
in the imagination a universal iridescence, a dithering of
presences and, say, a complex of differences" (*CPP* 858).
Elsewhere he offered the following:

> It is cosmic poetry because it makes us realize in the
> same way in which an escape from all our limitations
> would make us realize that we are creatures not of a
> part, which is our everyday limitation, but of a whole
> for which, for the most part, we have as yet no lan-
> guage. This sudden change of a lesser life for a greater
> one is like a change of winter for spring or any other
> transmutation of poetry. (*CPP* 856)

Against this background that Stevens so effectively re-
capitulated for his 1951 audience, he shaped his "rude aesthetic," replacing "empty heaven and its hymns" with "fitful
tracings"—"ditherings" iridescing in his imagination that
were nonetheless accurate descriptions of the relation between a man and his world, a *relation* fired with the full
charge of what William James delineated as "pure experience" and Stevens called a "radiant and productive atmosphere." The poet became—to borrow a felicitous phrase
from my dear friend and colleague Herwig Friedl, in his account of American modernist visionary thinking—"an aboriginal phenomenologist": "The modern thinker is in the
race of the aboriginal phenomenologist who allows the *un-
mediated* address of Being or nature or the world to make
itself felt as the defining challenge of all proper and authen-
tic thought."[3] Stevens, by his own account, was "like a man
lured on by a syllable without any meaning, / A syllable of
which he felt, with an appointed sureness, / That it contained the meaning into which he wanted to enter." Science
in the modern world, perforce, restored those who were
paying attention to "an original relation to the universe,"

what Charles Sanders Peirce called "Firstness": "What the world was to Adam on the day he opened his eyes to it, before he had drawn any distinction or had become conscious of his own existence—that is First, present, immediate, fresh, new, initiative, original, spontaneous, free, vivid, conscious, and evanescent."[4] "Throw away the lights, the definitions, / And say of what you see in the dark // That it is this or that it is that, / But do not use the rotted names."

Given the absolute but *natural* strangeness of the universe being disclosed as Stevens moved through the first half of the twentieth century, it is not surprising that he would find surrealism, as a movement and an aesthetic, to exhibit a failure of the imagination, an exercise in what Coleridge termed "Fancy" at best. As Stevens expressed in "The Noble Rider," "The imagination loses vitality as it ceases to adhere to what is real. When it adheres to the unreal and intensifies what is unreal, while its first effect may be extraordinary, that effect is the maximum effect it will ever have" (*CPP* 645).

It is important to underscore at this juncture the centrality of William James's work to the development of Stevens's thinking; we recall the poet noting in a late letter that during his time at Harvard the spirit of the philosopher permeated the atmosphere. In *Science and the Modern World*, calling James "that adorable genius," Whitehead suggested that James inaugurated a "new mentality," a "new stage in philosophy," "clear[ing] it of the old paraphernalia." Whitehead considered James's 1904 essay "Does 'Consciousness' Exist?" to be for the twentieth century what Descartes's 1637 *Discourse on Method* was for the seventeenth: he noted that James's contribution "mark[ed] the end of a period which lasted for about two hundred and fifty years" with his understanding, expressed in "Does 'Consciousness' Exist?" and generally throughout his work, that consciousness is *not an entity* or a "stuff" but a *function*, thereby correcting the Cartesian positing of two species of entities, *matter* and *soul*. Whitehead observed that both Descartes and James "open[ed] an epoch by their clear formulation of terms in which thought could profitably express itself at particular stages of knowledge, one for the seventeenth century, the other for the twentieth century."[5] Introducing the lectures that make up *Science and the Modern World*, Whitehead offered the following:

> The thesis which these lectures will illustrate is that [the] quiet growth of science has practically recoloured our mentality so that modes of thought which in former times were exceptional are now broadly spread throughout the educated world. . . . The new mentality is more important even than the new science and the new technology. It has altered the metaphysical presuppositions and the imaginative contents of our minds; so that now the old stimuli provoke a new response. Perhaps my metaphor of a new colour is too strong. What I mean is just the slightest change of tone which yet makes all the difference.[6]

"What I mean is just the slightest change of tone which yet makes all the difference": "as if the statement that every location involves an aspect of itself in every other location produced in the imagination a universal iridescence, a dithering of presences, and, say, a complex of differences." Whitehead continued to illustrate the demands made on the imagination and intellect with this shift by quoting from a letter William James wrote to his brother Henry as he was finishing his monumental *The Principles of Psychology* (1890): "I have to forge every sentence in the teeth of irreducible and stubborn facts." Whitehead then observed the following:

This new tinge to modern minds is a vehement and passionate interest in the relation of general principles to irreducible and stubborn facts. . . . It is this union of passionate interest in the detailed facts with equal devotion to abstract generalizations which forms the novelty in our present society. Previously it had appeared sporadically and as if by chance. This balance of mind has now become part of the tradition which infects cultivated thought. It is the salt which keeps life sweet.[7]

"Thought is an infection," Stevens observed. "In the case of certain thoughts it becomes an epidemic" (*CPP* 901). Thinking about "spooky action at a distance" has plagued physicists since the early twentieth century, when Einstein balked at believing it possible, but it has recently been proved. Our collective imagination was primed by the thinking about thinking of William James, Charles Sanders Peirce, quantum theorists, Wallace Stevens, and other poets and writers who were riding the crest of the wave breaking into our future. All exerted the fullest effort in forging their sentences in the teeth of the irreducible and stubborn but exquisite facts of the modern world.

5

THE SOUND OF WORDS

"The poet comes to words as nature comes to dry sticks" (*CPP* 909), Stevens set down in his *Adagia*, and we imagine his meaning: the poet animates words, gives them shape as they move us in their sounding. A man used to watching his intellectual processes, giving attention of the mind in thinking, Stevens would have known by practice what nineteenth- and early twentieth-century investigators of sound and its relation to words had discovered. In *The Principles of Psychology*, William James explicated and applied the findings of Hermann von Helmholtz, Carl Wernicke, and Paul Broca, among the most important early contributors to the study of wave properties and their extension into brain studies: "our ideas do not innervate our motor centers directly, but only after first arousing the mental sound of the words."[1] In *A Natural History of Pragmatism*, just after quoting James's observation, I described what is entailed in this understanding of the interplay between "linguistic formulations" and images in relation to Stevens's poetics:

> Verbal representations release action potentials, electrical pulses of individual arrangements, associations, stored pictorially, rebus-like. Stevens's repeated stress on the "sound of words" in his prose writings calls attention … to this central mechanism of mind,

certainly recognized experientially by Edwards and Emerson as well in their own reflective practice. The sound of a word, each time heard, whether vocalized or in silent rehearsal in reading or thinking, stimulates a different set of neural firings, the process releasing as much of the history of the word hidden in its metaphorical etymology as is known by a particular individual, intertwined with that individual's experiential, metonymical history of that word, the two strands connected by their changing combinations through and in time, the "occasions" of Whitehead and Stevens.[2]

"The slightest sound matters," Stevens wrote. "The most momentary rhythm matters.... You have somehow to know the sound that is the exact sound and you do in fact know, without knowing how.... There is, in short, an unwritten rhetoric that is always changing and to which the poet must always be turning" (*CPP* 789–90). This sensibility is the poet's particular gift, shared with the other animals that have learned to navigate in the dark: bats swerving in dark caves, or whales and dolphins swimming in dark seas. In the case of the poet this ability is often associated, properly, with mysticism, seeing in the dark of the mind: "*Muesis*, the closing of the eyes,—whence our word, *Mystic*," Emerson reminded us in "Swedenborg; or, The Mystic" (1850).[3] We know, of course, from our own experience how much more acutely we hear with our eyes closed; we are also more aware of our dimensionality in space and on the ground, feeling our way.

In *On Photography* (1977), which includes one of Stevens's aphorisms from *Adagia* in her "Brief Anthology of Quotations," Susan Sontag quoted in a footnote from Paul Valéry's 1929 "The Centenary of Photography." If photography discourages us from describing, he argued, we are thus reminded of the limits of language and are advised, as writers, to put our tools to a use more befitting their true nature. A literature would purify itself if it left to other modes of expression and production the tasks which they can perform far more effectively, and devoted itself to ends it alone can accomplish[,] … one of which [is] the perfecting of language that constructs or expounds abstract thought, the other exploring all the variety of poetic patterns and resources.[4]

Stevens was a great admirer of Valéry and shared his aesthetic. His direction for a "Supreme Fiction," *It Must Be Abstract*, underscores Valéry's remark here about the "perfecting of language" in "construct[ing] or expound[ing] abstract thought." Sound is, of course, the most abstract quality of language, "the most cognitively complex" of our sensory modalities, triggering, with its unalterable vibrations, the neuronal firings and circuitings that are the patterns we call thinking.[5] "The mind feels when it thinks," Jonathan Edwards observed as he set down notations of the images and shadows that emerged as he sounded his prayers.[6] "The slightest sound matters" and "all the variety of poetic patterns and resources" matter—become matter—as their sounds carry us back into an original relation with the universe, where we find ourselves in the situation of Firstness, reminding us that we are as strangers on the earth.

When, for example, Stevens in "Sea Surface Full of Clouds" carries us up and down in the rhythm of his lines again and again variously on "the perplexed machine // Of ocean," on "the tense machine // Of ocean," on "the tranced machine // Of ocean," on "the dry machine // Of ocean," and on "the obese machine // Of ocean," we are captured, captivated by, and held in the surface strangeness of his descriptions of the ocean as machine. We feel the sounds of the "night-long slopping of the sea" and the "night-long slopping of the sea [growing] still." The slopping followed by stillness prompts reflection *and* forms a figure of reflection, which at a moment of stillness comes to include a second-order reflection on the strangeness of using *machine* to describe the ocean. The practiced reader of Stevens, used to delving repeatedly into dictionary columns in search of "the hermit in [the] poet's metaphors" and to sounding the various meanings of a word, discovers that, originally for the Greeks and later for Lucretius, *mekhane*, *machina*, and *machina mundi* carried the meaning of being artfully contrived by a divine or supernatural being, "a contrivance that is both complex and purposeful, without that purpose being immediately transparent to the untrained eye." Moreover, this ur-meaning precedes the historical moment in which "the dualism of the organic and the mechanical" was established.[7] Thus, in sounding the history of a word that initially left us, like our object, "perplexed," we are indeed restored to Firstness, experiencing through our lexical excursion the reality of Emerson's observation in "The Poet" that "Every word was once a poem," a revelation of the reality of our being in language: men and women made out of words.[8]

There is another aspect of Stevens's profound understanding of how the sound of words extends the revelation of reality into modes and temporalities we ourselves might not have experienced; it belongs paradigmatically to "the cry of the peacocks" invoked hauntingly in "Domination of Black," an early poem that remained one of his favorites late into his career. Stevens described this poem as one of "sensation," specifically *not* "of ideas": "its sole purpose is to fill the mind with the images & sounds that it contains.…. You are supposed to get heavens full of the colors and full of sounds, and you are supposed to feel as you would feel

if you actually got all this" (*L* 251). The last stanza names
the feeling:

> Out of the window,
> I saw how the planets gathered
> Like the leaves themselves
> Turning in the wind.
> I saw how the night came.
> Came striding like the color of the heavy hemlocks.
> I felt afraid.
> And I remembered the cry of the peacocks. (*CPP* 7)

It is unlikely that a twentieth- or twenty-first-century
reader of or listener to the poetry of high modernism in
America would hear in the inner ear an echo of an actual
"cry of the peacocks." Yet an induced proleptic synesthesia
evokes the fear of ultimate darkening as we turn toward
death: the withered leaves falling and turning in the wind,
the color of the hemlocks deepening ominously in dimin-
ishing light. These conjurings of cosmic descent to noth-
ingness combine to elicit the *sensation* of "the cry of the
peacocks." For those who do one day come to hear the cry
in reality, as I did many years ago in an eleventh-century
monastery garden on the Greek island of Chios—an eerie
piercing shriek, an acrid desolate sound, the cry of death
itself, it seems—there is a chill of recognition, as though
the cry is actually remembered, their perception collapsed
into that of the poem's speaker, "all mean egotism vanished" once again. Those not encountering the sound in
reality remain suspended in its dark imagining, a prepara-
tory exercise.

6

Among the illuminating meditations in Susan Sontag's *On Photography* is a reflection on aspects of the emergence and development of this technology that are particularly useful in contextualizing the evolution of both Stevens's aesthetic and his ethic. The poet's life span coincided not only with Einstein's but also with the extraordinary proliferation of photographic images made possible by George Eastman's 1884 development of film to replace the photographic plate; by 1901, with the introduction of the Brownie, photography became available for the mass market. Sontag's final chapter, "The Image-World," opens with the following:

> Reality has always been interpreted through the reports given by images; and philosophers since Plato have tried to loosen our dependence on images by evoking the standard of an image-free way of apprehending the real. But when, in the mid-nineteenth century, the standard finally seemed attainable, the retreat of old religious and political illusions before the advance of humanistic and scientific thinking did not—as anticipated—create mass defections to the real. On the contrary, the new age of unbelief strengthened the allegiance to images. The credence that could no longer be given to realities understood

in the form of images was now being given to realities understood *to be* images, illusions.[1]

We recognize in Sontag's observations on "the new age of unbelief" echoes of what Stevens voiced in what was quoted from "Two or Three Ideas" and "A Collect of Philosophy" in the first chapter here. Her connection of this moment in the human condition with the function of the photographic image limns a backdrop against which to reconsider Stevens's self-appointed task to provide in a time of disbelief precisely what had once been provided—as he expressed in the letter to Elsie quoted earlier—by religious images. Yet noting as he did later that we live not in the time of Plato but in that of Darwin and Planck, when we know everything to be continuously changing, he understood that the nature of images had to be newly realized and processed. Stills, which could easily stand in for the "'idea' idea," had to be set in motion and in effect become *moving* pictures—flickering, "dithering," with the complex of feelings that attend our finding ourselves "dispossessed," as Stevens put it, including in that dispossession the realization of "disillusion" itself "as the last illusion."

I have quite deliberately chosen to omit the *The* from the name of the poem ("The Man on the Dump") that I have used as the title of this chapter. This is a way of looking at Stevens and his work, for which the poem's last line sets the scene: "Where was it one first heard of the truth? The the." One could easily use this poem as a metonym for the whole of Stevens's project; the second to fourth lines of the fifth stanza describe it starkly: "One beats and beats for that which one believes. / That's what one wants to get near. Could it after all / Be merely oneself." William James also called attention precisely to "The the," elaborating on a crucial insight made by his friend Charles Sanders Peirce. Here is what Peirce wrote about "The the":

[CHAPTER SIX]

A common mode of estimating the amount of matter in a MS, or printed book is to count the number of words. There will ordinarily be about twenty "the"s on a page, and, of course, they count as twenty words. In another sense of the word "word," however. there is but one word "the" in the English language; and it is impossible that this word should lie visibly on a page, or be heard in any voice, for the reason that it is not a Single thing or Single event. It does not exist; it only determines things that do exist. Such a definitely significant Form, I propose to term a *Type*.[2]

It was Peirce's investigation into the nature and behavior of language that produced his "Semeiotic," the groundbreaking theory of signs that underpins his pragmatism. Central to his understanding was the "recogni[tion] that science consists in inquiry, not in 'doctrine'—the history of words, not their etymology, being the key to their meanings, especially with a word so saturated with the idea of progress as science."[3] The crucial distinction between "the history of words" and "their etymology," of course, is *usage*, what the history of words traces. In Stevens's poem, "The dump is full / Of images." The dump is full of things once used, now thrown away.

Throw away the lights, the definitions,
And say of what you see in the dark

That it is this or that it is that,
But do not use the rotted names.

How should you walk in that space and know
Nothing of the madness of space,

Nothing of its jocular procreations?
Throw the lights away. Nothing must stand

Between you and the shapes you take
When the crust of shape has been destroyed.

"The the," the crust of shape.

In "Does 'Consciousness' Exist?"—the essay that White-head noted as marking the beginning of the modernist moment as Descartes's *Discourse on Method* had laid the groundwork for the Enlightenment—James offered one of his clearest explications of "pure experience," the basis of the "radical empiricism" on which his *Pragmatism*—as text and method—rests. James described what he exqui-sitely termed "the rhapsody of our successive thoughts":

> The instant field of the present is at all times what I call the 'pure' experience. It is only virtually or poten-tially either subject or object yet. For the time being, it is plain, unqualified actuality or existence, a simple *that*. In this *naïf* immediacy it is of course *valid*; it is *there*, we *act* upon it; and the doubling of it in retro-spection into a state of mind and a reality intended thereby, is just one of the acts. The 'state of mind,' first treated explicitly as such in retrospection, will stand corrected or confirmed, and the retrospective experience in its turn will get a similar treatment; but the immediate experience in its passing is always 'truth,' practical truth, *something to act on*, at its own movement.[4]

It is precisely to this impalpable friction that Stevens attended—"only virtually or potentially either subject or object yet"—and that he transcribed in his poems. It was the fruit of giving close attention of the mind in thinking, the active interface between the "true subject" and "the poetry of the subject" that he named and illustrated in his 1936 Harvard lecture, "The Irrational Element in Poetry." This interface is a moving picture of mind as activity, as *minding*. This activity is perfectly captured by James's term "rhapsody," which has its root in the Greek *rhapto*, to sew or stitch together; it came into its later use because of the way the ancient Greek poets "stitched" together the sections of the tales they recited to their hungry listeners. The salient feature of their extraordinary skill, emblematized in the attribution of blindness to Homer, is that in order to have been able to hold in memory and deliver episodically the orally received and transmitted epic, these rhapsodists simultaneously engaged visual-spatial and aural capacities. They *were*, in other words, *the song they sang*, in *pure experience*, seeing in the dark of their mind's eye the scene they were singing.

Serendipitously, in the days I was composing these last pages—in fact, between the time I set down the first two sentences of the paragraph just above and what follows—I received in the mail the fall 2015 issue of *The Wallace Stevens Journal*, a special number given to "Stevens and the Cognitive Turn in Literary Studies." In it Mark J. Bruhn offers a brilliantly insightful and valuable analysis of the poet's pervasive deployment of various forms of chiasmus: phonetic, lexical, grammatical, conceptual, stanzaic, and linear, as well as combinations thereof (i.e., phonetic-lexical and conceptual-stanzaic). Bruhn points out that chiasmus is an embodied, preconceptual "image schema," a *pattern*—in this case *abba*—that arrests "attention upon an inherently non-semantic relation of parts"; in Stevens's phrase, "an unwritten rhetoric."[5] As indicated by the title of his piece, "A Mirror on the Mind: Stevens, Chiasmus, and Autism Spectrum Disorder," Bruhn discusses this prominent stylistic feature of Stevens's poetry in the context of findings concerning preverbal and verbal information processing and the brain's bilateral symmetry; the image schema of chiasmus in particular is "naturally motivated by the bilateral symmetry of our bodies and especially our nervous systems."[6] Bruhn's point is not to claim that Stevens was on the autism spectrum, but—far more important, as I see it—to give the clue to the great power of his poetry: Stevens was able to access the pre-verbal, visual-spatial aspects of minding at the same time as the verbal—in the same way, I suggest, as the ancient Greek rhapsodists.

There is not space in this volume to present all the details of Bruhn's tracing; I strongly urge readers to consult Bruhn's excellent contribution for themselves. There are, however, a few of his observations and research findings that are too useful not to be included in the present reading.

Drawing on the work of "the late Max Nanny, a Swiss-born scholar of English and American literature, who . . . analysed chiasmus in linguistic and neurological terms" and found that "the chiastic patterning *abba* may occur not just on the sentence level but on *all* levels of a literary text," Bruhn provides a table illustrating the varieties of chiasmus in Stevens's verse. He observes that "given that chiasmus can operate at any level of the linguistic and literary systems, its formal pattern is evidently neither linguistic nor literary, but . . . visual-spatial." He further notes Nanny's speculation that "linguistic chiasmus ought to have a distinctive neural signature." As it turns out, "chiasmus is not a mere linguistic feature learned through exposure to literary discourse but rather a pre-linguistic cognitive pattern, or even neural disposition, grounded in the bilateral, mirror-symmetrical organization of the visual cortex."[7] This feature of the visual cortex is what is responsible for the difficulty we all have as children, when learning the alphabet and writing words and names, in confusing left and right, printing *s* backward, for instance, or *d* for *b*. (Individuals on the autism spectrum cannot override this natural proclivity for mirror imaging in the brain, a function lodged in the neural circuiting of the occipito-temporal cortex and originally evolved for predominantly visual-spatial purposes, such as recognizing familiar patterns on paths through a landscape.)

Bruhn continues, referring to the research of neuroscientist Stanislas Dehaene concerning reading and the brain, "With years of reading and writing practice, most children's brains overcome this inborn bias for generalization 'across mirror orientations,' not by *pruning* mirror-symmetrical pathways to the right occipito-temporal cortex but instead by learning simply to ignore them." But according to Dehaene, "The mirror [is] not broken, but merely hidden."[8] Drawing from Dehaene and other researchers on the enhanced pattern detection capacities of this aboriginal system, Bruhn comments on Stevens's ability to superimpose "something of the mind's own form upon ... linguistic experience":

> Stevens's poems hew formally to pre-linguistic and pre-conceptual patterns whose origins lie in the very sensorimotor capacities that afford us "the direct pleasure provided by objects," including language in its material dimensions. Understood in this deep cognitive rather than merely ornamental sense ... rhetorical schemes, and chiasmus preeminently, provided Stevens with a crucially self-reflexive scaffolding for the poetic disposition of an otherwise stubbornly falsifying (because merely conceptual and therefore inescapably metaphorical) language system.[9]

In attending to this "'prehistorical, preconceptual, and prelinguistic' dimension of human cognition itself[,] ... in particular 'the manner in which experience is actually sensed, in the blaze of all of its affect and meaning-laden intensity,' prior to its translation into language-mediated conceptual sense," Stevens sounded the "recesses of feeling, the darker, blinder strata" of experience which are, as William James described, "the only places in the world in which we catch real fact in the making, and directly perceive how events happen, and how work is actually done."[10] (In the next chapter, "Darken Your Speech," we will revisit aspects considered here in particular connection with the signal pleasures and nourishment preserved in language's primitive, chthonic elements.)

William James not only called attention to these archaic levels of human being but also pointed out that what we ordinarily refer to as consciousness does not really exist; it is, rather, as noted earlier, a synthetic function, a function of *minding*'s multilevel processing, with each level registering information and pulsing at its own rate. The present "thought"—"which is called I"—is the articulated composite, strained or sorted through various sieves to a rationed, rational purpose, most often appetitive.[11] Whereas Freud divided the psyche into three registers, James suggested that there are several—each of our senses, for example, responding to a different bandwidth of wave vibrations. In this connection, let us return to "The Man on the Dump" and consider it as a meditation on the classical sorites paradox, the paradox of the *heap*—the name given to a class of arguments that arise as a result of the indeterminacy surrounding limits of a predicate's application—the problem of "The the," in other words. A heap is used as the illustration because when we designate something as a heap, no one item can be identified as *the one* that makes a difference between the items being a heap and not being a heap. According to the *Stanford Encyclopedia of Philosophy*, "the phenomenon at the heart of the paradox is . . . vagueness."

James stated that his chief aim in *The Principles of Psychology* was "the re-instatement of the vague to its proper place in our mental life."[12] He set this as his aim because of all he had come to know about our situation in the cosmos, awash amidst and permeated by wave currents arranged in energy fields—knowledge just beginning to be observed and studied in the nineteenth century. Fluent in German and French, James used the word *vague* pointedly, deploying its meaning in French as "wave": the complex and multiply erratic manifestations the sea takes on in interaction with winds and the earth's rotation, as opposed to *onde*, the concentric rise and fall of water around some weight dropped into it. "The Man on the Dump," paradigmatically—and all of Stevens's poems, in fact—records the activity of minding with the vague reinstated to its proper place; that is, what he registered throughout the course of his lifetime was the actual straining of the manifold "up-pourings" (a word coined by Stevens) from the deep recesses of being through the machine of "a stubbornly falisifying language system."

It is no surprise that so much of Stevens's poetry remains opaque: he was transcribing the vague—what James otherwise called "the fringe" accompanying and informing each "thought"—the interplaying currents out of which and with which perception emerges: "a most chaotic pure experience which sets us questions." In fact, "reality is an accumulation of our own intellectual inventions, and the struggle for 'truth' in our progressive dealings with it is always a struggle to work in new nouns and adjectives while altering as little as possible the old."[13] Just as Beethoven, though already deaf when composing his last sonatas on a newly designed six-octave piano, expanded the tonal and dynamic range of the instrument by feeling his way, improvising from one register to another in wayward harmonies and syncopated rhythms, Stevens expanded the tonal and syntactic range of poetic language by chording, superpositioning metaphorically, multiple levels of *minding* along the sentential staff. His brilliantly innovative technique interrupts and slows the metonymic sliding of predication by creating backwashes and eddies, extending in the thought experiments of his poems "the instant field of the present ... 'pure' experience ... [still] only virtually or potentially either subject or object," before "The the."

7

DARKEN YOUR SPEECH

"Insistence on clarity at all costs is based on sheer superstition as to the mode in which human intelligence functions," Whitehead observed.[1] Stevens experienced this actuality acutely as he moved up and down between his lawyerly practices and those demanded by poetry. Equally apt is Emerson's observation from "Poetry and Imagination," an essay Stevens certainly knew: "God himself does not speak prose, but communicates with us by hints, omens, inference and dark resemblances in objects lying around us."[2]

In the preface to *The Demon and the Angel*, Edward Hirsch provides both useful context and keen insight concerning the chthonic aspects of poetic engagement. As he remarks, "Art is born from struggle and touches an anonymous center. Art is inexplicable and has a dream-power that radiates from the night mind. It unleashes something ancient, dark, and mysterious into the world." Hirsch's offering here, he notes, was in response to discovering Federico García Lorca's lecture on *duende* ("All that has dark sounds has *duende*"), which Hirsch pairs with Emerson's "The Poet" as capturing the essence of the human trajectory in and through time as expressed by "the artistic night-mind." Hirsch particularizes, "One finds it [*duende*] in works with powerful undertows. It surfaces wherever and whenever a demonic anguish suddenly charges and electrifies a work of art in the looming presence of death"— "like a duet with the undertaker," in Stevens's phrasing from "The Man with the Blue Guitar," the title itself evoking a figure strumming *duende*'s plangent chords.³ Although Stevens referenced Lorca only late in his career—using a line from him in "The Novel" and noting its provenance in a letter to Tom McGreevy on August 25, 1950—it is clear he shared the Spanish poet's sense of *duende*, evoking what Stevens described as "all the breathings / From the edge of night": "Those dark sounds are the mystery, the roots that cling to the mire that we all know, that we all ignore, but from which comes the very substance of art ... in sum the spirit of the earth."⁴

Specifically concerning Stevens's embrace of the dark elements of experience—composing, as it were, the music for a modern *danse macabre*—it is important to keep in mind the cultural and political events against and amid which the writing of his mature poetry began. Stevens's early years of roaming New York City's streets at night were filled by sounds coming from piano bars and honky-tonk saloons downtown and in Harlem where African American musicians—part of the mass migration to northern cities during the last quarter of the nineteenth and first years of the twentieth centuries—transposed the plaintive blues notes, syncopated rhythms, exotic temperaments, and cadences drawn from spirituals, work songs, and ring shouts into their new urban settings:

> There are these sudden mobs of men,
>
> These sudden clouds of faces and arms,
> An immense suppression, freed,
> Their voices crying without knowing for what,
>
> Except to be happy, without knowing how.

All these elements found their way into Stevens's sonic lexicon beginning with his first collection in 1923, *Har-*

monium, where their variety is most pronounced; there they provided the basic vocabulary from which he would develop the themes and variations of his "Grand Poem," "The Whole of Harmonium." It is not surprising that Carl Van Vechten—the music and dance critic for the *New York Times* who, convinced that "Negro culture was the essence of America" and who "put the blues on a par with Beethoven"—was, according to Stevens, "the *accoucheur*" (midwife) of the volume; Van Vechten had persuaded his friend Alfred Knopf of the exceptional quality of Stevens's ear and voice and of the poet's temperament in scaling new, exotic ranges of experience.[5] (Van Vechten "was celebrated, in retrospect, as one of America's first major dance critics, and one of the first music critics to embrace the sounds of the twentieth century."[6])

During the early years of Stevens's career there was also, of course, the great darkness of World War I and its aftermath. No one captured its impact as bluntly, perhaps, as Ezra Pound: "There died a myriad, / And of the best, among them, / For an old bitch gone in the teeth, / For a botched civilization / ... For two gross of broken statues, / For a few thousand battered books."[7] While Pound and T. S. Eliot in England were close enough to the trenches to see the red glow from firing and grenade blasts hang in the night air across the Channel, on this side of the Atlantic, news from the front provided a vivid backdrop for the decline and decay already manifest in the still young nation before the catastrophe of the Great War. In *Wisconsin Death Trip* (1973), Michael Lesy constructed with the aid of photographs a portrait of the rural country between 1890 and 1910, precisely the period in which Stevens came of age and witnessed the increasing destruction of pastoral life in and around Reading. Referring to Lesy's work, Susan Sontag observed, "In case anyone was thinking that it was Vietnam and all the domestic funk and nastiness of the past decade which had made America a country of darkening hopes, Lesy argues that the dream had collapsed by the end of the last century—not in the inhuman cities but in the farming communities; that the whole country has been crazy, and for a long time."[8] It was in this post-Reconstruction landscape that Stevens traveled over the next decades, surveying, in his capacity as an insurance claims lawyer, the deconstruction of the American dream before it ever became a reality: "the thought of what America would be like"—stillborn.[9]

At the same time, in the face of the terrible facts of World War I, the gorgeous ("gawdy," in Stevens's locution [*L* 263]) language passed down through chronicles of conquest—from the linguistic acquisitions brought with the Normans in 1066 that would enliven the speech of the Elizabethans to "the music and manner of the paladins" celebrated by the Victorians—had to be purged of its idealism. Paeans of praise for heroes spilling noble ribbons of blood for God and country had to be replaced with bare dark facts describing the results of a technology that was itself a product of the Enlightenment's dream of reason but that left millions of young men wounded and slowly rotting to death in stinking trenches. Paul Fussell's *The Great War and Modern Memory* (1975) documented most fully the impact and lingering effects of this terrible event on language, literature, and thinking in English. Had it not been for the invention of the camera, of course, and (by the time of the Great War) its extension into the moving pictures of newsreels, it might have been possible to preserve the lie of a worthy and august cause warranting the massacre of so many. But the eye of the cameraman could not justify what the eye of God once could have. ("I grow tired of the want of faith," Stevens wrote.) And while Fussell foregrounded memory in his title and discussed the way that the big picture of what was called "the war to end all wars" would provide the background against which the following acts of the first half of the twentieth century would play out, he did not focus on the changes in the actual process of memory in consequence of the culture's having effectively to erase, or at best short-circuit, an entire vocabulary of being—what Stevens called "abstraction[s] blooded" by over seven million dead, "a hoard of destructions."

When thinking, speaking, and writing about national aspirations and values, the progress of history, or virtues like bravery, honor, and valor, anyone touched by the war, rather than being able to reflect and almost automatically retrieve words and concepts in place for hundreds of years, would find instead that being at a loss for words returned memory to its default mode as it went into a tailspin (random access working in overdrive, as it were) to fill discursive gaps as quickly as possible. It is not surprising that dadaism began when it did. The disruption of the lines of rational communication brought with World War I ironically did bring liberation—from worn-out habits of mind long trained by words and concepts no longer valid: "Regard the invalid personality / . . . outcast, without the will to power / And impotent, like the imagination seeking / To propagate the imagination or like / War's miracle begetting that of peace." The culture was out of breath and almost out of its mind in trying to keep up with time passing ever more quickly. Out of the dense violent night of war came Stevens's directive: "Darken your speech."

8

I have purposely continued to thread references to photography through these ways of looking at Stevens and his work because its own ways of seeing so dramatically changed our relation to all aspects of the world and to ourselves, most strikingly and coincidentally, as noted earlier, during Stevens's life span. John Berger, one of the astutest critical historians of the form, noted, "Marx came of age the year of the camera's invention. It was not, however, until the twentieth century and the period between the two world wars that the photograph became the dominant and most 'natural' way of referring to appearances. It was then that it replaced the word as immediate testimony." Berger connected photography with the emergence of the advertising industry during roughly the same period, then asked, "Has the camera replaced the eye of God? The decline of religion corresponds with the rise of the photograph."[1]

As we reflect back on Stevens as a young man already mourning the "want of faith" and wishing that there were something still sacred, Berger's contextualization of this event in modern time is especially illuminating:

It is necessary to recognize that the intolerability of the world is, in a certain sense, an historical achievement. The world was not so intolerable so long as

God existed, so long as there was the ghost of a pre-existent order, so long as large tracts of the world were unknown, so long as one believed in the distinction between the spiritual and the material (it is there that many people still find their justification in finding the world intolerable), so long as one believed in the natural inequality of man.[2]

The cultural impact and importance of the development of photography and its offshoots—color prints, newsreels, documentaries, and motion pictures—cannot be overstated; indeed, its significance in changing habits of mind and behavior equals that of the personal computer and its offshoots: the World Wide Web, handheld devices, and remote-controlled robots of various kinds. Stevens was a regular participant in the gatherings of what came to be known as the Arensberg Circle, a group of avant-garde artists and writers brought together between 1914 and 1921 in the spacious West 67th Street apartment of Louise and Walter Arensberg (the latter a contemporary and friend of Stevens's at Harvard). Stevens was among those who, taking their cue from the Arensbergs, followed the issues of Alfred Stieglitz's *Camera Work* as they appeared more or less quarterly until 1917, when the journal ceased publication; the Arensbergs also made available to their friends all past issues of the journal, which began in 1903.

Although the primary focus of *Camera Work* was not overtly political, it documented both the fact and feeling of the American scene simply because its images and articles reflected the changing landscape and population during its years of publication—for example, the contrast between Stieglitz's romantic rendering of the Flatiron Building and Paul Strand's later, starker shots of the city or of Stieglitz's famous "Steerage." On a more profound but not immediately apparent level, the formal qualities of the photograph and its presentation established the modernist aesthetic while capturing (albeit incidentally) an essential aspect of the nature and behavior of memory. Concerning the formal properties of photography, in a 1909 issue of *Camera Work* Stieglitz noted the undeniable influence of photography on painting, an influence that should be extended to poetry. As Susan Sontag observed, "The assumption underlying all uses of photography, *that each photograph is a piece of the world*, means that we don't know how to react to a photograph (if the image is visually ambiguous: say, too closely seen or too distant) until we know *what* piece of the world it is."[3] The title of Stevens's 1942 volume, *Parts of a World*, takes this aesthetic shift in stride, for his sensibility had been primed early on by the experimental uses of photography exemplified in *Camera Work*.

The uses of photography deployed by those, like Stieglitz, who realized it as an art broke with the practice of setting realistic images unilinearly to illustrate an argument or demonstrate a thought, understanding instead that photographs could capture the seemingly random processing of memory. Rephrasing (though without referencing) William James's findings contained in *The Principles of Psychology*, Berger observed, "Memory is not unilinear at all. Memory works radially ... with an enormous number of associations.... Memory is a field where different times coexist. The field is continuous in terms of the subjectivity which creates and extends it, but temporarily [*sic*] it is discontinuous."[4] Berger reminded us that for the ancient Greeks, "Memory was the mother of the Muses, and ... most closely associated with the practice of poetry. Poetry[,] ... being a form of storytelling, was also an inventory of the visible world[;] metaphor after metaphor was given to poetry by way of visual correspondence."[5]

Photography released from its illustrative or objective

documentary purposes has actually functioned, then, as an *aide-mémoire*, representationally reminding us to give attention to making the invisible visible—that is, providing a sense of "the more than rational distortion" of experience and events as they come to be stored in the neuronal structure and firing. Through this technology the matter of mind itself became the subject. As Sontag noted:

> The ethos of photography—that of schooling us (in [Laszlo] Moholy-Nagy's phrase) in "intensive seeing" seems closer to that of modernist poetry than that of painting.... Poetry's commitment to concreteness and to the autonomy of the poem's language parallels photography's commitment to pure seeing. Both imply discontinuity, disarticulated forms and compensatory unity: wrenching things from their context (to see them in a fresh way), bringing things together elliptically, according to the imperious but often arbitrary demands of subjectivity.[6]

We should remember here the work of Henry Fox Talbot (1800–1877) in mid-nineteenth-century England, with his 1834 experiments on salted paper using sunlight as "The Pencil of Nature," which preceded Louis Daguerre's first forays in 1839. The emergence of Talbot's photography more or less coincided with that of *psychology*, the term that took the place of *mental philosophy*, especially in the work of William Hamilton (1788–1856). In "Philosophy of the Unconditioned," which appeared in the *Edinburgh Review* in 1829, Hamilton laid down the principle that *every object is known only in virtue of its relations to other objects*; in this he prefigured William James.

Given this twin historical birth, it does not seem at all strange that the terms used to describe the processes of dreamwork—*distortion, displacement, condensation, am-*

biguity, and *symbolism*—also characterize the primary elements of the aesthetics of photography understood as an art. The complementarity of inner worlds and external images profoundly changed habits of mind. Edward Weston observed, "Once they began to think photographically, people stopped talking about photographic distortion."[7] "Photography gave a tremendous boost to" what Sontag called "the cognitive claims of sight, because— through close-up and remote sensing—it so greatly enlarged the realm of the visible," with X-rays even seeing through matter.[8] All of the aspects introduced with photography and later extended into film—such as montage, panning, cuts, fades, zooms, and stop-motion—added wildly to the tool kits of modernist poets and writers before becoming new moving parts of the grammar and syntax of twentieth-century culture. Stevens was on the cusp of this new way of seeing and understood its usefulness as a metaphor for exploring "the border of the question of the relationship of the imagination and memory" (*CPP* 681). Scrutiny of the unseen became a primary focus for this secular priest of the invisible.

Stevens was fascinated from boyhood with light in all its variety and mystery. He chose rooms facing west for his combined bedroom and study in the house on Westerly Terrace in Hartford, Connecticut, where he and his wife eventually settled, because, as he expressed in a letter to a friend, he was always trying to get his windows facing in the same direction as those in his childhood room; he wanted to experience ordinary evenings with shadows that would evoke memories of his early years. As evidence of his preoccupation with light and the constant slow turning of the earth, the image glaringly preponderant in his *Collected Poems* is that of the sun with its light changing evening into night; of the 301 poems, 107 name or describe the sun or some indication of the diurnal rhythm. Moreover, in the same way that Jonathan Edwards (another longtime inhabitant of the Connecticut Valley) used all he learned about the nature and behavior of light from his close readings of Isaac Newton's *Optics* as the primary figure describing the nature and behavior of grace, Stevens used light as the primary figure for describing imagination.[9] He spelled out this equivalence in "The Figure of the Youth as Virile Poet," first delivered as a lecture at the Entretiens de Pontigny Conference at Mount Holyoke College in August 1943 and later published in *The Necessary Angel*. After noting that "much of the world of fact is the equivalent of the world of the imagination," which brings us to the "border … of the imagination and memory," he continued:

> Poetry is the scholar's art. The acute intelligence of the imagination, the illimitable resources of its memory, its power to possess the moment it perceives—if we were speaking of light itself, and thinking of the relationship between objects and light, no further demonstration would be necessary. Like light, it adds nothing, except itself. What light requires a day to do, and by day I mean a kind of Biblical revolution of time, the imagination does in the twinkling of an eye. It colors, increases, brings to a beginning and end, invents languages, crushes men and, for that matter, gods in its hands, it says to women more than it is possible to say, it rescues all of us from what we have called absolute fact. (*CPP* 681)

After commenting that photography provided a tool for "the focusing of a temperament" that could be extended to other ways of knowing, Sontag recalled Moholy-Nagy's observation in a 1936 essay that "photography creates or enlarges eight distinct varieties of seeing: abstract, exact, rapid, slow, intensified, penetrative, simultaneous, and distorted."[10] One could usefully apply each of these aspects to Stevens's poetic transformations of "the exquisite environment of fact" under the power of imagination—like light, adding nothing but itself.

9

ORDINARY EVENING

> O thin men of Haddam,
> Why do you imagine golden birds?
> Do you not see how the blackbird
> Walks around the feet
> Of the women about you?

This is the eighth of Stevens's "Thirteen Ways of Look-ing at a Blackbird." It focuses on one of the basics of his "rude aesthetic," something else he learned from Emerson, as noted earlier, that was reinforced by what he learned from "the old Chinese . . . by their mountain pools": that the extraordinary is to be found in the ordinary, and that an essential part of the poet's work is shaping and turn-ing words so that they bring to light the miraculous in the everyday—like turning a piece of labradorite to find its transparent brilliance, as Emerson described. In the intro-duction to *The Necessary Angel* Stevens quoted himself from a recent lecture and continued, "[Poetry] is an illu-mination of a surface, the movement of a self in the rock. A force capable of bringing about fluctuations in reality in words free from mysticism is a force independent of one's desire to elevate it. It needs no elevation. It has only to be presented, as best one is able to present it" (*CPP* 639–40). Stevens knew from experience how vital this exercise is. In

the absence of a belief in God or gods, being able to participate in what the Beatles would later call the "magical mystery tour"—attending in detail to the immense strangeness
of existing on a planet spinning on its axis at 1,040 miles
per hour (at the equator) while simultaneously revolving at
67,000 miles per hour around an aging low-mass star on
whose energy all life on earth depends—provides a secular
sense of the sacred. In opening "The Irrational Element in
Poetry," Stevens used an ordinary memory to begin to ex-
plore the idea of writing "poetry to find the good which, in
the Platonic sense, is synonymous with God":

> A day or two before Thanksgiving we had a light fall
> of snow in Hartford. It melted a little by day and then
> froze again at night, forming a thin, bright crust over
> the grass. At the same time, the moon was almost
> full. I awoke once several hours before daylight and
> as I lay in bed I heard the steps of a cat running over
> the snow under my window almost inaudibly. The
> faintness and strangeness of the sound made on me
> one of those impressions which one so often seizes as
> pretexts for poetry. (*CPP* 781–82)

Stevens's use of "pretexts" here alerts us to his attending to that archaic, prelinguistic, animal register of being
discussed in chapter 6. "The faintness and strangeness of
the sound" situated him in pure sensation—the level of
embodied cognition even deeper, more primal than that
of emotions, which are instinctual reactions experienced
and reexperienced over eons to become humans' second
nature, as it were. Learning to attune ourselves to the level
of sensibility we share with all animate creatures exponentially expands our sense of earthly commonality. At the
same time multiple dimensions of perception are added
to ordinary experience as we are properly reminded of our
"bond to all that dust." In "The Figure of the Youth as Vir-

ile Poet," Stevens spoke eloquently of the "radiant and productive atmosphere" created and inhabited by the poet:

> The indirect purpose or, perhaps, it would be better to say, inverted effect of soliloquies in hell and of most celestial poems and, in a general sense, of all music played on the terraces of the audiences of the moon, seems to produce an agreement with reality. It is the *mundo* of the imagination in which the imaginative man delights and not the gaunt world of the reason. The pleasure is the pleasure of powers that create a truth that cannot be arrived at by the reason alone, a truth that the poet recognizes by sensation. The morality of the poet's radiant and productive atmosphere is the morality of the right sensation. (*CPP* 678–79)

Although *radiant* is generally used to describe light or heat—and certainly Stevens was intent throughout this essay to elaborate the metaphor of light as imagination—black bodies also radiate, as do sound waves and all waves on the electromagnetic spectrum (including, as we have recently learned, the gravitational waves that Einstein imagined and predicted in 1913). Tuning to frequencies below and above "normal" thresholds, to frequencies and vibrations without names, registering additional spatiotemporal dimensions, this acute sensitivity along with with loving words—"In poetry, you must love the words, the ideas and images and rhythms with all your capacity to love anything at all" (*CPP* 902)—constitute the poet's special gift. Becoming so finely tuned is the poet's work, persistently illuminating the magic of words, our most common and ordinary tools. Stevens observed:

> The slightest sound matters. The most momentary rhythm matters. You can do as you please, yet every-

thing matters. You are free, but your freedom must be consonant with the freedom of others. To insist for a moment on the point of sound … You have somehow to know the sound that is the exact sound; and you do in fact know, without knowing how. Your knowledge is irrational. In that sense life is mysterious; and if it is mysterious at all, I suppose that it is cosmically mysterious…. What is true of sounds is true of everything: the feeling for words, without regard to their sound, for example. (*CPP* 789–90)

Words are thoughts and not only our own thoughts but the thoughts of men and women ignorant of what it is that they are thinking … poetry is words; and … words, above everything else, are, in poetry sounds. … A poet's words are of things that do not exist without the words. (*CPP* 663)

Earth's atmosphere, the medium accounting for the blueness of what we call the sky, is composed of the continuous exhalations of all living matter on the planet; *atmos* means "steam" or "vapor." In our case this is the breath accompanying each exhalation and voicing:

In the anonymous color of the universe.
Our breath is like a desperate element
That we must calm, the origin of a mother tongue

With which to speak to her.

The atmosphere, in other words, is our exchange with the cosmos. It was an essential part of Stevens's understanding of the work of poetry to make us aware of this ordinary miracle. In closing "The Figure of the Youth" he offered the following:

Poetry is the imagination of life. A poem is a particular of life thought of for so long that one's thought

has become an indispensable part of it or a particular of life so intensely felt that the feeling has entered
into it. When, therefore, we say that the world is a
compact of real things so like the unreal things of
the imagination that they are indistinguishable from
one another and when, by way of illustration, we cite,
say, the blue sky, we can be sure that the thing cited
is always something that whether by thinking or feeling has become part of our vital experience of life,
even though we are not aware of it. It is easy to suppose that few people realize on that occasion, which
comes to all of us, when we look at the blue sky for
the first time, that is to say: not merely see it, but
look at it and experience it and for the first time have
a sense that we live in the center of a physical poetry,
a geography that would be intolerable except for the
non-geography that exists there—few people realize that they are looking at the world of their own
thoughts and the world of their own feelings. On that
occasion, the blue sky is a particular of life that we
have thought of often, even though unconsciously,
and that we have felt intensely in those crystalliza-
tions of freshness that we no more remember than
we remember this or that gust of wind in spring or
autumn. The experiences of thinking and feeling
accumulate particularly in the abnormal ranges of
sensibility. (*CPP* 684)

Once we begin to get used to attending to "the abnormal
ranges of sensibility" offered in Stevens's poems, something extraordinary happens to the way we experience. The
range of our own sensibilities stretches to pick up signals
we would not otherwise have registered: "The mobile and
immobile flickering / In the area between is and was." Just
one excellent example will serve: "An Ordinary Evening in

New Haven," the poem invoked in this chapter's title and from which I have quoted above. There is not space here for a full close reading; I will dwell briefly on only two elements playing against each other in the title, a counterpoint that is the clue to how to read, what to do in engaging not only this poem but any Stevens poem.[1]

Although the poem's title names a time of day in the Connecticut city that is home to Yale University (where, it is to be noted, Jonathan Edwards's spirit is still palpable), "An Ordinary Evening" also evokes a particular sound. It is a sound familiar to those who are, as Stevens was, interested in and knowledgeable about ecclesiastical music: the sound of one or more parts of the Ordinary of a Mass *evening* into faintness. (There are five parts: the Kyrie, the Gloria, the Credo, the Sanctus or Benedictus, and the Agnus Dei.) The Ordinary is of particular historical significance, as noted by a musicologist specializing in the Mass, "occupy[ing] a central place in the output of each generation of anthologized composers from Bach to Poulenc and beyond. The pedagogical appeal of the Ordinary is self-evident: the text of a Kyrie by Machaut is the same as that of a Kyrie by Mozart or by Stravinsky."[2] In other words, the Ordinary tells time with the sound of its music. In the same way, as Stevens elaborated in "The Noble Rider and the Sound of Words," the sound of a poet's words—the decrescendo of denotation into connotation, as he indicated—locates him in his particular spatiotemporal range.

For the listener in the imagined now of the speaker of "An Ordinary Evening," the knowledge that it was composed for the occasion of the 1949 jubilee meeting of the Connecticut Academy of the Arts and Sciences flutters as a necessary angel through, above, and below the lines. The academy, attached to Yale, was founded in 1799 by Timothy Dwight IV (the grandson of Jonathan Edwards; he was known as Pope Dwight and was its eighth president), Noah Webster Jr. (of the first *American Dictionary* [1828] fame), Benjamin Silliman (who gave the first science lectures at Yale), and Ezra Stiles (its first president; he established Semitics at Yale and required students to study Hebrew). The spirits of these studious ghosts and so many more (such as Edwards, who was an original member, and all the noted speakers over two and a half centuries) hovered in the poet's mind as he put together what he would offer that ordinary evening in New Haven. Two others were also invited to celebrate the academy's sesquicentennial meeting: Paul Hindemith, who would conduct a specially composed piece for trumpet and percussion reflecting his abiding interest in celestial movements and "cosmic drama"; and the scientist Max Delbruck, who had been a student of Niels Bohr and whose lecture for this evening, "A Physicist Looks at Biology," underlined the affinity between poets' and scientists' use of language. Delbruck vividly evoked the unique situation of any living organism against the cosmic background: "the key problem of biology, from the physicist's point of view, is how living matter manages to record and perpetuate its experiences."[3]

For Stevens it was the entire range of his imagined experience, stretching through time—back through Edwards and the other theologians of New Haven all the way to "A figure like Ecclesiast," and forward to a future where it would be possible to conceive that "It is not in the premise that reality / Is a solid" but rather "a shade that traverses / A dust, a force that traverses a shade"—that constituted the present (the "specious present" James described as "pure experience") of his stanzas, the rooms of his idea, "Like an evening evoking the spectrum of violet." By the time we get to the end of the poem, *evening* does not, and never will again, simply denote a time of day, nor will *ordi-*

nary be ordinary. Ever after we will feel the *spell* of evening in the everyday changing of light into darkness—an ordinary magic has allowed us to see through words.

It was evening all afternoon.
It was snowing
And it was going to snow.
The blackbird sat
In the cedar limbs.

10

PLANET ON THE TABLE

Just opening Stevens's *Collected Poems* and scanning the titles alerts readers new to his work that this was indeed a man in the habit of conversation with nature:

"Earthy Anecdote"
"Sea Surface Full of Clouds"
"Stars at Tallapoosa"
"Of the Manner of Addressing Clouds"
"Lunar Paraphrase"
"In the Clear Season of Grapes"
"Indian River"
"To the Roaring Wind"
"Snow and Stars"
"The Sun This March"
"A Fading of the Sun"
"A Postcard from the Volcano"
"Autumn Refrain"
"A Fish-Scale Sunrise"
"Delightful Evening"
"The Poems of Our Climate"
"A Weak Mind in the Mountains"
"The Blue Buildings in the Summer Air"
"Dezembrum"
"Of Hartford in a Purple Light"
"Forces, the Will & the Weather"

"Variations on a Summer Day"
"Yellow Afternoon"
"Of Bright & Blue Birds & the Gala Sun"
"The News and the Weather"
"Transport to Summer"
"Credences of Summer"
"The Auroras of Autumn"
"This Solitude of Cataracts"
"A Primitive like an Orb"
"Our Stars Come from Ireland"
"Things of August"
"One of the Inhabitants of the West"
"The Rock"
"Note on Moonlight"
"The River of Rivers in Connecticut"
"The Region November"
"July Mountain"

Then, going slowly through the poems, readers realize that they are accompanying the spirit of this man through the seasons and years of his life and, moreover, that his attention moved gradually up from the earth and the things of earth, identifying with its parts ("I wish that I might be a thinking stone") to rise through the atmosphere as one of the elements of weather, finally to circulate in and with the "celestial pantomime" itself, as "Ariel," regarding himself in the end with "cosmic consciousness" as a physical specimen, a "planet on the table":[1] "He looked in a glass of the earth and / thought he lived in it. // Now, he brings all that he saw into the earth, to the waiting / parent."

Of course, one who attends to moving through the cycles of nature will find an invisible element in addition to light entering the scene: time, the fourth dimension, so prominent a feature of the world's preoccupation during Stevens's lifetime. In 1889 Henri Bergson had already elaborated on the difference between subjective psychological time and objective time: *la durée* versus *le temps*. But dealing with Einstein's correct prediction that time as well as space curves—that time passes more quickly higher up than at ground level—was almost too much for the mind to grasp. In his recently published and lucid primer *Seven Brief Lessons on Physics*, Carlo Rovelli offers an example of what this finding means: "If a person who has lived at sea level meets up with his twin who has lived in the mountains, he will find that his sibling is slightly older than he. And this is just the beginning."[2] Perhaps Stevens's "musing the obscure" possibilities resulting from this discovery, confirmed in 1919, was the prompt for "A Weak Mind in the Mountains," where the poem's speaker records "meeting" this kind of stubborn fact: it "gripped my mind, / Gripped it and grappled my thoughts. / ... The blood of the mind fell / To the floor."

Ludwig Wittgenstein, ten years Stevens's junior but witness to the same seismic shift in perception, culture, and values, observed, "It is not 'how' things are in the world that is mystical, but that it exists."[3] The philosopher's remark expresses the attitude the poet was intent to document in constructing his own language game, in which his readers must become players if they are to understand the stakes and have a chance of "winning," which in this game means (to borrow one of Emerson's descriptions of imagination) gaining "a very high sort of seeing ... the intellect being where and what it sees ... sharing the path, or circuit of things through forms, and so making them translucid to others"—making the invisible visible, in other words.[4] Let me explain, beginning with the salient terms to be considered: *attention*, *document*, *mystical*, and *play*.

In an age of disbelief, with the notion of God or the gods having disappeared, never to return, it is no longer possible to call on an account of how things came to be. Moreover, as John Archibald Wheeler—the noted Princeton University theoretical physicist who popularized the term *black hole*—put it, we inhabit a "universe that is far stranger and more beautiful than we realize," but we cannot perceive it in its beauty and simplicity "until we first realize how strange it is." In our early twenty-first-century moment, we who are secular have become somewhat used to, if not complacent about, accepting the uncertainty concerning the origin of the universe and the strangeness of it all. But it is important to emphasize that this late human condition of suspended possibility of belief and of incomprehension concerning the cosmos was new cultural territory during the first half of the twentieth century and that—taking into full account Wittgenstein's notation of the wild situation in which we exist—Stevens meant to record what it felt like *to be in the very difficulty of what it is to be*: "It was a shift / Of realities." For all practical purposes, he was a participant observer in the newly discovered culture of space-time: documenting, taking notes, looking for patterns, and mapping new schemata of thinking in this exotic locale. Herwig Friedl's descriptive phrase for the American visionary writer as "aboriginal phenomenologist" comes to mind here, as does an observation by John Banville in a recent review of Tom McCarthy's *Satin Island*. After commenting on the need "human creatures" have to believe in some kind of larger ordering principle, "in gloriously irresponsible denial of the cold reality staring them in the face," Banville continues:

> The *nouveaux romanciers*, along with a few lone giants such as Wallace Stevens—phenomenologists to a man and woman, whether they knew it or not— considered that the only solution must be to turn back to the thing, the *Ding* if not quite the *Ding an sich*, and refuse to be distracted by mere chatter-

ing: the *thing*, that is, and not our notions of it, the pathetic fallacy banished for good. As Stevens beautifully put it in "Notes Toward a Supreme Fiction": "The sun / Must bear no name, gold flourisher, but be / In the difficulty of what it is to be."[5]

For Stevens, documenting the *thing* stripped of any ideas about the thing included regarding any word as thing, *pragma*, artifact, construction, a provisional "stay against chaos." In the same way that an anthropologist attempts as much as possible to remain neutral in recording observations in order to be able to understand *functions* simply and clearly—as William James came to understand consciousness as a *function*—so Stevens cultivated a scrupulous and dispassionate attention to the full spectrum of each word's sound and sense in its strangeness, its Firstness, and allowed the lines of his stanzas to compose themselves as word games, thereby priming his readers to become equally attentive to finding themselves in language as if on a newly discovered planet. A good example is the first stanza of "Forces, the Will & the Weather":

> At the time of nougats, the peer yellow
> Sighed in the evening that he lived
> Without ideas in a land without ideas,
> The pair yellow, the peer.

What is this? As an aid to orienting themselves, readers may recall lines from "Notes Toward a Supreme Fiction":

> From this the poem springs: that we live in a place
> That is not our own and, much more, not ourselves
> And hard it is in spite of blazoned days.
>
> We are the mimics. Clouds are pedagogues ...
>
> Looking for what was, where it used to be ...

The poem goes from the poet's gibberish to
The gibberish of the vulgate and back again.

These lines from "Notes" seem helpful, describing somewhat the situation in which readers find themselves; the
lines are discursive, not "gibberish" because the subjects
and scenes are recognizable, just as the second and third
lines of "Forces, the Will & the Weather" are. But it is the
scene—"the time of nougats"—with its subject—"the peer
yellow"—that cause confusion that only deepens in the
fourth line with what appears to be an attempt at clari-
fication: "The pair yellow, the peer." The last lines quoted
just above from "Notes" seem to be describing what is hap-
pening in this stanza if the reader understands the first
line to be "the poet's gibberish," then the second and third
moving back to what is acceptable—"the gibberish of the
vulgate"—and then "back again" in the fourth line to "the
poet's gibberish." "The "gibberish of the vulgate" is a tip-off.

   Through his play on and with words—which are, after
all, only *things*, like the balls kept in the air by a juggler (or
jongleur, a medieval figure who not only juggled but also
played with words)—Stevens was calling attention to the
force holding the words together, keeping them *in play*,
seeming on the surface like sense; the force, of course,
is grammar. In *Twilight of the Idols* Friedrich Nietzsche
offered a brilliantly incisive observation that is apt here.
Properly expressed as a *fear*—although the word appears
to be simply part of an idiomatic phrasing, in German as
well as in English—he wrote, "I fear that we are not getting
rid of God because we still believe in grammar."[6]

   Complementing (or, perhaps better, informing) Nietzsche's aperçu—behind which might have been Emerson's equally troubling notation in "The Poet" that "Every
thought is also a prison"—is William James's alert to the
vulnerability of sense to grammatical structure.[7] In "The

Stream of Thought" chapter of *The Principles of Psychology*, James offered the following:

> Usually the vague perception that all the words we hear belong to the same language and to the same special vocabulary in that language, and that the grammatical sequence is familiar, is practically equivalent to an admission that what we hear is sense. But if an unusual foreign word be introduced, if the grammar trip, or if a term from an incongruous vocabulary suddenly appear, such as 'rat-trap' or 'plumber's bill' in a philosophical discourse, the sentence detonates, as it were, we receive a shock from the incongruity, and the drowsy assent is gone.

James continued by quoting the following from a French contemporary, M. G. Tarde, writing on sleep and dreams: "Even when awake, *it is more difficult to ascend to the meaning of a word* than to pass from one word to another." After including in his main text some examples that on careful reading prove to be hilarious—illustrating how easily grammar seduces readers into believing they have understood the meaning of a text, and then noting, "There are every year works published whose contents show them to be by real lunatics"—James concluded, "To sum up, certain kinds of verbal associate, certain grammatical expectations fulfilled, stand for a good part of our impression that a sentence has a meaning and is dominated by the Unity of one Thought. Nonsense in grammatical form sounds half rational."[8]

Stevens set traps in the midst of the apparent orderliness of his stanzas, like Berserk setting traps in the midst of dreams in "Anecdote of the Prince of Peacocks." There are many, and even though I have been reading Stevens closely since the late 1960s, I am sure I have not yet found them all. "Dry Birds Fluttering in Blue Leaves" did not catch me for years, and when the switching of the adjectives from their expected places finally caught my attention, I also recognized the closeness of the phrase to one of the examples used by James in "The Stream of Thought" discussion: "The birds filled the tree-tops with their morning song, making the air moist, cool, and pleasant."[9]

Whether Stevens also remembered James's illustration is immaterial: what does matter is that readers learn to play the game, sharpen attention, and become wary as they move around in language, alert to the constraints grammar imposes on perception. (I cannot help thinking of Stevens in his role as "Comedian" with an aspiration for "angelic hilarity" (*L 101*) and the game played by Peter Sellers as Inspector Clouseau learning to hone his detecting skills through the games played with his servant Cato.) "The field cannot be well seen from within the field," Emerson gnomically warned in "Circles."[10] It is necessary to fly up, to ascend ("The river is moving. / The blackbird must be flying"): "for there never can be a state of facts to which new meaning may not truthfully be added, provided the mind ascend to a more enveloping point of view. It must always remain an open question whether mystical states may not possibly be such superior points of view, windows through which the mind looks out upon a more extensive and inclusive world."[11] Gradually ascending, spiraling out in ever larger circles through the years of his life, taking "the temperature of heaven," Stevens came to achieve cosmic consciousness, the secular form of mystical experience, identifying with the sun—"All things in the sun are sun"—and with light itself: "The mind between this light or that and space." "The thing I hum appears to be / The rhythm of this celestial pantomime."

A world without God needs a new grammar. Charles Darwin revised *On the Origin of Species* six times, attempting with each revision to get rid of the idea of design, or teleology. In *Nature* Emerson, as Oliver Wendell Holmes was the first to note, had anticipated the theory of evolution even before Robert Chambers's *Vestiges of Creation*. With the stochastic structure of his essays and lectures, Emerson attempted to align the "axis of vision" of his readers and listeners to the life of "this planet ... cycling on according to the fixed law of gravity" and producing "endless forms most beautiful and most wonderful."[12] Stevens, taking up Emerson's charge "to follow so far those shining laws ... see them come full circle ... see the world to be the mirror of the soul ... the identity of the law of gravitation with purity of heart," composed his poems as lessons in learning a new uncertain and strange grammar.

II

IT CAN NEVER BE SATISFIED, THE MIND, NEVER

Rising up, "up—and—ho," out of language ("No doubt we live beyond ourselves in air") and regarding it from above, as a specimen, like "the planet on a table," invites probing and exploring it, tinkering, experimenting, and seeing what happens if this word or that is moved here or there or omitted altogether. This is precisely what Stevens did in his language games. Indeed, this kind of play characterizes the work of major poets, no matter the period. Think of John Milton's telescoping sentences lexically imitating inversely the effects of Galileo's simple yet extraordinary invention—Milton's setting the subject of a sentence, for example, at its end, so the reader has to extend the sense and movement of the predicate through seven, eight, or nine lines. Or think of Lucretius, so many centuries before, describing the nature and behavior of atoms. Milton's verse then inspired Charles Darwin in his findings, and Lucretius's, Niels Bohr. This reciprocal relation of poets and natural philosophers, or scientists, derives from their shared engagement with imagination—Emerson's "very high form of seeing," using it to develop cosmic consciousness, as I have been tracing.

John Tyndall, a nineteenth-century Irish physicist, lectured and wrote eloquently about imagination in this connection. In 1870 he delivered a lecture, "The Scientific Use of Imagination" (later published and reprinted widely), which opened with excerpts of poetry from Emerson and from Goethe, in which Tyndall spoke of the "prepared imagination."[1] Tyndall knew from his own experience that what Samuel Taylor Coleridge called "the esemplastic power of the poetic imagination" belonged also to scientists who projected the visual into thought experiments— *Gedankenexperiment*—like (James Clerk) Maxwell with his "demon," Einstein chasing a light beam, or (Erwin) Shrödinger with his cat. In creating hypothetical scenarios the "prepared imagination" adds itself as another, sixth, sense: "Add This to Rhetoric"—"In the way you speak / You arrange, the thing is posed, / What in nature merely grows."

Whitehead formalized the word *prehension* to indicate this sense. Coupled with what he beautifully described as the "appetite of thought," he theorized the activity of mind to be as actual an organic process as respiration or digestion and as autonomic as those functions. In rendering the work of the intellect in this way, he was following the lead of his "adorable genius," William James, who in opening his foundational "Stream of Thought" chapter, observed that it would be far more accurate to express what happens in the mind by saying "it thinks" rather than "he or she thinks." ("If we could say in English 'it thinks,' as we say 'it rains' or 'it blows,' we should be stating the fact most simply and with the minimum of assumption."[2]) The difference between a poet or a scientist and the greater number of "ordinary" women and men is that the poet and the scientist have learned to attend to *it*: "A man conversing in earnest, *if he watch his intellectual processes*, will find that a material image, more or less luminous, arises in his mind, contemporaneous with every thought." The trick, in other words, is, to learn to give close "attention of the mind in thinking," to follow it in its flights and perchings.

Henry James observed the following in connection with his own reading of Tyndall:

> "The mind," he [Tyndall] excellently says . . . "is, as it were, a photographic plate, which is gradually cleansed by the effort to think rightly, and which, when so cleansed, and not before, receives impressions from the light of truth." This sentence may serve at once as a . . . text for remark on the highly clarified condition of . . . intellect. The reader moves in an atmosphere in which the habit of a sort of heroic attention seems to maintain a glare of electric light.[3]

A fine example of the product of admitting "the prepared imagination" as a sense, of *prehension*, of watching how it shapes or reshapes what the eye sees in the service of truth, is Charles Lyell's use of his imagination to realize how many more millions of years beyond the then-projected (in the early 1800s) three hundred million it had to have taken for the earth in its revolutions around the sun to have acquired its many geological strata as residual evidence. The results of his thought experiment then became one of the bases on which Darwin was able to continue the experiment and understand that given the eons earth had existed, it was possible for human beings to have evolved from "a hairy quadruped mostly arboreal in its habit," and organic life itself from the primordial soup bubbling in rocky star-warmed pools.

Stevens's early memorandum to himself, "Look not *at* facts, but *through* them," reflected his awareness of the habits of attention of the visionary company investigating and measuring "the verve of earth." It is important to note that measuring in one way or another and multiple times is an intrinsic activity of mind: rationality is the constant sifting with increasingly finer-gauged sieves the elements encountered in experience to discover which is like which. The greater the discriminations perceived, the more finely tuned the creature to the myriad aspects of its environment: "It can never be satisfied, the mind, never." In "Swedenborg; or, The Mystic" Emerson observed the following:

> The mind is a finer body, and resumes its functions of feeding, digesting, absorbing, excluding, and generating, in a new and ethereal element. Here, in the brain, is all the process of alimentation repeated, in the acquiring, comparing, digesting, and assimilating of experience. Here again is the mystery of generation repeated. In the brain are male and female faculties: here is marriage, here is fruit. And there is no limit to this ascending scale, but series on series. Every thing, at the end of one use, is taken up into the next, each series punctually repeating every organ and process of the last. We are adapted to infinity … in nature is no end. … Creative force, like a musical composer, goes on unweariedly repeating a simple air or theme, now high, now low, in solo, in chorus, ten thousand times reverberated, till it fills earth and heaven with the chant.[4]

Today, as neuroscientists have recently documented, we know that what we know as conscious mind is only 2.5 percent of the continuous and simultaneous processing on multiple registers of *it* thinking. (Scientists have determined that at any moment our five senses are taking in more than eleven million pieces of information and that by the most liberal estimate we can process about forty pieces per second.[5])

It was to the greatest extent the work of William James (which began to be adequately acknowledged only in the past generation) that alerted those paying attention to the different rhythms of the multiple registers of mind and to the inadequacy of language as its instrument—particularly English and the Germanic languages with their preponderant substantive forms—to catch these pulses that nonetheless express their meanings within us:

> As we take … a general view of the wonderful stream of our consciousness, what strikes us first is this different pace of its parts. Like a bird's life, it seems to be made up of an alternation of flights and perchings.
>
> If there be such things as feelings at all, *then so surely as relations between objects exist in rerum natura, and more surely, do feelings exist to which these relations are known.…*
>
> We ought to say a feeling of *and*, a feeling of *if*, a feeling of *but*, and a feeling of *by*, quite as readily as we say a feeling of *blue*, a feeling of *cold*. Yet we do not, so inveterate has our habit become of recognizing the substantive parts alone, that language almost refuses to lend itself to any other use.… All *dumb* or anonymous psychic states have, owing to this error, been cooly suppressed; or, if recognized at all, have been named after the substantive perception they led to, as thoughts 'about' this object or 'about' that, the stolid word *about* engulfing all their delicate idiosyncrasies in its monotonous sound. Thus the greater and greater accentuation and isolation of the substantive parts have continually gone on.[6]

To begin to access these ranges of experience pulsing below and beyond the ordinary thresholds of perception requires recalibrating our instruments: we need a wider broadband receiver, as it were, the grammar and syntax of our language expanded to allow reception of the complex harmonies and chordings of the multiple simultaneous receptors and rhythms of the mind's life. As James pointed out, for any moment of consciousness, "language works against our perception of the truth." He continued, "We name our thoughts simply, each after its thing, as if each knew its own thing and nothing else. What each really knows is clearly the thing it is named for, with simply perhaps a thousand other things. It ought to be named after all of them, but it never is."[7] To represent the actual situation in the brain, James offered as an example, in place of the subject of a sentence, a series of subscript letters, a, b, and c, rising arpeggio-like below the space of the subject: "three different processes coexisting, and correlated with them a thought which is no one of the three thoughts which they would have produced had each of them occurred alone."[8] (We think of Stevens's "I was of three minds, / Like a tree / In which there are three blackbirds.") These resonant frequencies vibrate with all that cannot yet be articulated within the rules of the language as it is—"we have as yet no language." Nonconceptual superpositionings and suggestions of visuality, as well as associations of temporality, "ditherings," accompany each and every predication, the undertones and overtones of every color of the mind. Stevens began making necessary adjustments, within his various experiments, refashioning language into a finer instrument.

It was noted earlier that light in its various manifestations is Stevens's preponderant image. In this connection we should not forget, as Hans Blumenberg has reminded us, that "the metaphor most closely linked to the problem of truth" is "the metaphor of *light*," which in itself explicates the question of truth "in a concealed plenitude never yet hazarded by any system."[9] Words naming light in some form or shade—in which, of course, colors have to be included, as well as effects of weather—constitute more than one-quarter of Stevens's lexicon, in counterpoint to the sun, which, as noted above, is named or referred to in more than one-third of the poems. The first sentence of "Lebensweisheitspielerei"—a title tipping us off to the poet's gaming—announces "Weaker and weaker, the sunlight falls / In the afternoon," preparing us for the twilight mood of evening, but even more particularly forecasting the mood as characterizing "Little by little, the poverty / Of autumnal space."

James Turrell, who is thought by many to be the greatest artist of our time, was reared a strict Quaker. His medium is light, and he is preternaturally sensitive not only to the interstices of existing tones but also to those of possible tones; he has, for example, created more vibrant, lucent whites by combining seven or more tones in place of the usual three (red, green, and blue). He uses these different "whiter" whites in an astronomical program called "twilight compression" for changing the projected light in his sky spaces depending on the duration of twilight through the seasons as the earth orbits the sun: twilight is equal at the equinoxes, then lengthens until the summer solstice and shortens as the winter solstice approaches. Stevens, "acutest poet," was clearly alert to this phenomenon, measuring out his life not in coffee spoons but in the degrees of light falling into his study as part of the "planetary passpass": "the memory of a certain fulmination or declension of light that was unique to that time and that place on that day."[10] How to live, what to do—it matters what you pay attention to. A mind entrained to "the exquisite environment of fact" will tune its instrument to the temperament of the cosmos, thereby increasing the shadings of meaning exponentially: "We are adapted to infinity."

12

IMAGINATION AS VALUE

In 1895 William James read and was impressed by Swami Vivekananda's *Raja-Yoga*; they had met in 1894, and in March 1896 Vivekananda delivered an address to the Graduate Philosophical Society at Harvard on "The Philosophy of Vedanta." James later described Vivekananda as "an honor to humanity." Vivekananda had been speaking widely in the United States since 1893, when he first presented his ideas at the Parliament of Religions held as part of the Columbian Exposition in Chicago. He was from a high-caste family, was deeply educated and cosmopolitan, and intended to integrate "evolutionism" into Hinduism and, reciprocally, introduce the West to the teachings of the East. In his "Practical Vedanta, Lectures on Jnana Yoga" (the yoga of the mind), Vivekananda observed that most of our differences as human beings "are merely differences of language."[1]

James shared this notion. Pragmatism, as conceived by Charles Sanders Peirce and developed by James, is a method designed to show *how to make our ideas clear* (the title of one of Peirce's foundational pragmatist essays): the basis of the method is learning to attend to the many possible shades of meaning in the words we use. Imagination's value in this mental scanning is to perform spectrum analyses, considering the meaning and "feeling of *if* " in this context, "of *and*" in another, or of "around" in the famous example of the squirrel and the tree used by James in his *Pragmatism* (1907). Peirce had been in the habit since childhood—having been trained by his father, the Harvard astronomer and mathematician Benjamin Peirce—of recording star measurements and adjusting carefully by degrees for parallax distortion. He carried this skill over to the way he imagined words in their different usages. This exacting attentiveness to the varieties of verbal experience characterized Stevens's way with words as well, and he composed his poems as exercises to teach us, women and men made out of words, how and what to do with them: "The slightest sound matters." By reading through Stevens's body of work we learn to become pragmatists.

In chapter 1 I remarked that as Stevens developed his poetics, certain lessons that he took in from the East, beginning during his years at Harvard, were to become as formative as what he internalized from his native West. The young poet was sensitized to nuance early in his life from reading Emerson, and as he came to know the art and poetry of the East when it became the subject of exhibitions and scholarship in Boston and Cambridge (Ernest Fenollosa's collection and lecturing being the wellspring), he found his senses excited even more by the delicacy of distinctions and the shape or schema of ideas. He read Chinese and Japanese aesthetics. In a letter to Elsie in the months before they married, he transcribed lists of colors drawn from things he had seen and of "aspects" that could be used to compose paintings or poetry: "pale orange, green and crimson, and white, / and gold, and brown"; "deep lapis-lazuli and orange, and opaque / green, fawn-color, black, and gold"; and "lapis blue and vermilion, white, and gold / and green." And he transcribed the following list of aspects:

The Evening Bells from a Distant Temple
Sunset Glow over a Fishing Village
Fine Weather after Storm at a Lonely Mountain Town
Homeward-Bound Boats off a Distant Shore
The Autumn Moon over Lake Tung-t'ing
Wild Geese on a Sandy Plain
Night Rain in Hsaio-Hsiang

He commented as follows:

> This is one of the most curious things I ever saw, be-
> cause it is so comprehensive. Any twilight picture is
> included under the first title, for example. "It is just
> that silent hour when travellers say to themselves,
> 'The day is done,' and to their ears comes from the
> distance the expected sound of the evening bell."–
> And last of all in my package of strange things from
> the East, a little poem written centuries ago by Wang-
> an-shih: "It is midnight, all is silent in the house; the
> water-clock has stopped. But I am unable to sleep
> because of the beauty of the trembling shapes of the
> spring-flowers, thrown by the moon upon the blind."
> I don't know of anything more beautiful than that
> anywhere, or more Chinese— ... I am going to poke
> around more or less in the dust of Asia for a week or
> two and have no idea what I shall disturb and bring
> to light.—Curious thing, how little we know about
> Asia, and all that. It makes me wild to learn it all in
> a night. (*L* 137–38)

Throughout his life Stevens continued learning more
about Asia, Buddhism, and the life of the Buddha, eventually building his own small collection of statues of the
Buddha. It is particularly useful in the context of what has
been so far presented in this penultimate way of looking
at Stevens to draw from the work of Nolan Pliny Jacob-

son, the noted scholar of Buddhism in its affinities with American pragmatism. An observation Vivekananda made repeatedly to his audiences in America is pertinent as well: the Buddha was a Hindu, the first to bring Vedanta out of India. Jacobson's insight is especially helpful in relation to Stevens's understanding of imagination as value. Here, then, is Jacobson focusing on Peirce's affiliation with Buddhism:

> For Peirce . . . all thinking is dialogic in nature, extending the feeling of the thinker into the feelings of others—this is what he means by the "outreaching identity" of the self. What distinguishes the human mind is not that it is unextended—nothing really is, Gilbert Ryle's "ghost in the machine" notwithstanding. What distinguishes the mind is the acuteness of its sensitivity to the shared processes of feeling and the equally distinctive ability to extend the range of our awareness by high-level sign language, "by knowing which," Peirce says, "we know something more" and engage in dialogue with private and public moments in our experience. This is crucial for Peirce's philosophy of science, as well as an access road into profound dialogue with the Buddhist orientation. "There is an immediate community of feeling between parts of mind infinitesimally near together, between the self at one moment and the oncoming self of the next; without this," Peirce writes, "it would have been impossible for minds external to one another ever to become coordinated in the search for public truth to which even the most prejudiced persons will come if they pursue their inquiries far enough."[2]

Peirce's aim, shared by James and inherited by Stevens, was to use language "to strengthen and multiply the connective links that establish human life more firmly in its natural habitat, rendering more transparent our relations with one another and with the speechless world's fellow-creatures."[3] "Remember how the crickets came / Out of their mother grass, like little kin, / In the pale nights, when your first imagery / Found inklings of your bond to all that dust?"

In one of his meditations on the function of the photograph in the modern period, John Berger underscored that the ever increasing acceleration of events does violence to human experience. "The violence consists in conflating time and history so that the two become indivisible, so that people no longer read their experience of either of them separately." Writing in 1982, he continued with a description especially chilling in relation to where we find ourselves today (as I write in 2016):

> The conflation began in Europe in the nineteenth century, and has become more complete and more extensive as the rate of historical change has increased and become global. All popular religious movements—such as the present mounting Islamic one against the materialism of the West—are a form of resistance to the violence of this conflation.
>
> What does this violence consist in? The human imagination which grasps and unifies time (before imagination existed, each time scale—cosmic, geological, biological—was disparate) has always had the capacity of undoing time. This capacity is closely connected with the faculty of memory. Yet time is undone not only by being remembered but also by the living of certain moments which defy the passing of time, not so much by becoming unforgettable but because, within the experience of such moments there is an imperviousness to time. They are experi-

ences which provoke the words *for ever, toujours, siempre, immer.* Moments of achievement, trance, dream, passion, crucial ethical decision, prowess, near-death, sacrifice, mourning, music, the visitation of *duende.* To name some of them.

Such moments have continually occurred in human experience. . . . They are the material of *all* lyrical expression. . . . They are summit moments and they are intrinsic to the relation imagination/time.[4]

Stevens wrote as follows:

The imagination is the power of the mind over the possibilities of things ... it is the source not of a single value but of as many values as reside in the possibilities of things. (*CPP* 726)

The imagination that is satisfied by politics, whatever the nature of the politics, has not the same value as the imagination that seeks to satisfy, say, the universal mind, which in the case of the poet, would be the imagination that tries to penetrate to basic images, basic emotions, and so to compose a fundamental poetry even older than the ancient world. (*CPP* 732)

And, as coda, again:

It is not an artifice that the mind has added to human nature. The mind has added nothing to human nature. It is a violence from within that protects us from a violence without. It is the imagination pressing back against the pressure of reality. It seems, in the last analysis, to have something to do with our self-preservation; and that, no doubt, is why the expression of it, the sound of its words, helps us to live our lives. (*CPP* 665)

13

THE IMPERFECT IS
OUR PARADISE

The title of this final chapter, a line from "The Poems of Our Climate," is one of the parts of Stevens's world that kept returning in my early involvement with him and his work, "up-pouring" unbidden at this moment or that—as have the two lines from "Thirteen Ways" that I used as the epigraph for this volume, and there are others. Each of these extracts has come to serve as enigma and lesson or, more precisely, lesson as enigma: whenever arising, prompting me to quiz it. Often I have to recall or reread the poem from which it comes until I discover the message it is carrying—a necessary angel, indeed—a message that in some way shows me what to do at these moments. When I read Harold Bloom's remark, quoted earlier, that Stevens had helped him to live his life, I knew exactly what he meant.

Unlike "The river is moving. / The blackbird must be flying," whose precise location, even the position of the lines on the page in the different editions of Stevens's poems, has become part of my hardwiring, when "The imperfect is our paradise" sounds in my mind's ear and I need to cite its locus, I have to search, first trying to place it in its poem by memory, then, if failing to find it where I thought I would, searching the text either by going through pages to note my underlinings and marginal marks or, if pressed for time, resorting to the online Stevens concordance. This last move is always dissatisfactory because its quick solution forecloses my once again having to play the hunting game, to reenter Stevens's territory to track my quarry through his forest of words. I should add that I am drawn into this same kind of game by lines of Emerson's that I also know by heart but can't place without tracking: "Conversation is a game of circles" and "The field cannot well be seen from within the field," for instance—even, as in the case of the latter, when I have already quoted and cited it in a text I am composing. I find these occultings fascinating and provoking. Indeed, in the same way that reading and decoding the occultings of the beam of light in a lighthouse permits those at sea to navigate to their desired harbors, reading and decoding these moments in Stevens and Emerson leads me to a spiritual haven, a resting place of insight.

In mentally gathering some of these elusive riddles and reflecting on them, I find their common feature to be that each can stand alone as a gnomic utterance that reveals itself, after a bit of reflection, as a truism; the reflection, however, requires an imaginative engagement, a deliberate prehension requiring spatial and/or temporal amplification. I will explain in a moment. Let me first note that because these kinds of statements can stand alone as apothegms, not requiring a context to explain or locate them (unlike the descriptions of the blackbird, which locate themselves automatically in their memorial contextual nest) accurately re-placing the gnomic offerings requires re-searching their contexts; their places have to be found again and again—it was lost but now is found, to paraphrase a familiar biblical verse.

Moreover, the gnomic value of these offerings is that they provide self-reflexive observations of aspects of *minding*, of thinking, the most elusive of all beasts in the jungle of being. It does not seem to me accidental that either Emerson or Stevens set these postings in their fields. Rather, my

[CHAPTER THIRTEEN]

sense is that they expected that those coming after them and hunting their spirits would periodically have to walk through their pages again and again, following blazes to find them in the places that particular thoughts, seemingly simple yet of profoundest weight, revealed themselves. "The poet seems to confer his identity on the reader" (*CPP* 901): "this thought which is called *I*."

In these closing pages I will focus on "The imperfect is our paradise," since, after all, it is Stevens who is the subject of this volume, but my observations on the nature of the mental activity prompted by this statement apply equally to the examples from Emerson. In functioning both as a line within a stanza in "The Poems of Our Climate" and as self-standing apothegm, "The imperfect is our paradise" is at the same time particular and universal. This collapse of individual into general confers truth value on the individual statement and allows it to stand as a beacon, a signal in the "sea of spuming thought." Recognizing the difference of this kind of statement from the others around it means that the reading mind is performing a first-order reflection on the relationship between language and thinking, an activity that depends on having grasped, or prehended, the schema of thought, a prehension that is both visual and spatial, if abstract. This kind of seeing is, to paraphrase one of the items of Stevens's *Adagia*, like glimpsing a pheasant disappearing in the brush. The experience of this kind of *reading* makes us keenly aware of how difficult thinking really is and reminds us, too, that "to read" originally meant "to advise," to provide some guidance about how to live, what to do. Relearning to pay attention to the seeing that subtends, that is the ground of, saying returns us to the basic slate of being in relation to the world and language: we begin our lives "without words," the literal meaning of "infant," from the Latin *in-fans*. ("Infancy is the perpetual Messiah, which comes into the arms of fallen men, and pleads with them to return to paradise," wrote Emerson in *Nature*.[1]) Gradually these thoughts that are called *I*s are made out of words, shaped by and in the language into which we happen to be born; we are *of it*, yet in using it we can never perfectly capture all the frequencies of being that are registering: "The imperfect is our paradise." The imperfect is our human condition—"speaking together" from the Latin *condicere*—our climate.

In choosing his words for this singular line, Stevens was also drawing on "the imperfect" as the French verb tense describing uncompleted, ongoing action, a tense that exists only *imperfectly* in English, parsed between the past progressive—*I was writing*—and the form using an auxiliary—*I used to write*. The imperfect verb in French, *j'écrivais* (and analogously in the other languages in which it has a definite form), is expressed in one word, so it carries a sense impossible to render in English; the single-word phrasing more closely mimics the situation of the subject being identical with or emerging from the *verbing*, the activity of being in words. The imperfect, that is, preserves an originary and essential feature of the human condition in language that can otherwise easily become obscured. In this reminding, the imperfect is close to the middle voice, another aspect that has been lost in English and most modern languages but that belonged to Sanskrit as well as to Classical Greek and survives in Demotic Greek and some Slavic languages. The middle voice, Herwig Friedl notes, "allows us to envision the action or a state of affairs as preceding and determining the subject involved in it." Moreover, "the middle voice tends or tended to subordinate the noun subject to an event preceding, co-determining, and possibly affecting it without transforming the subject into a mere recipient as, e.g., in the case of the passive voice." The middle voice, like the imperfect, "places a process at the center of the world,"[2] a process that is ongoing, with the subject part of, not separate from, the activity: "And when she sang, the sea / Whatever self it had, became the self / That was her song." It is historically and ontologically significant that the middle voice receded from the Indo-European languages as subject-object dualism took over. To help repair this fatal split and restore us to "an original relation to the universe" was Stevens's aim, even if only in momentary existence on that exquisite plane.

Finally, to repeat an earlier observation, it matters what you pay attention to. Stevens's poetry is "a cure of the mind," "a health," not only because it persistently extends "the compass and curriculum" of our thinking and imagining to feel ever more deeply the human "bond to all that dust," but also because its difficulty demands that we wrestle with it—as a necessary angel, bringing to bear all our powers of minding, powers that include not only concentration but also emptying. In 1958 Louis Martz published what was to become a classic essay, demonstrating the closeness in structure of Stevens's poems to seventeenth-century English poems of meditation in their drawing on religious exercises for clearing the mind. Around the same time Frank Kermode observed that this manner extended as well into Stevens's prose pieces: "These essays are constructed like meditative poems, circling beautifully around central images, proceeding with a grave gaiety to repetitive but ever-changing statements about the imagination."[3] In my own critical biography of the poet (two volumes, 1986 and 1988), I discussed Stevens's disjunctive manner of titling poems in connection with the riddling aspect of Zen koans, Eastern exercises in meditation, both techniques meant to prompt conceptual emptying—"an interval in the life of the mind"—in preparation for witnessing the mind as it engages itself: "Nothing that is not there and the nothing that is."[4]

Stevens's poems are exercises in meditation, designed to loosen inherited, outworn habits of thought inappropriate to honoring the life of all things on the planet of which we are a part. For those of us in the West, perhaps the most insidious is the idea of progress, currently operating as the "utopian, millenarian faith" of neoliberalism.[5] Arthur Schopenhauer—as John Gray has recently reminded us, "the first major European thinker to know anything about Indian philosophy"—alerted his readers to how subtly the Christian myth of Providence transformed itself into Enlightenment notions of progress and human exception from nature.[6] Stevens began reading Schopenhauer in 1905 and significantly incorporated his ideas concerning the nature and function of imagination, drawn as they were from Vedantic sources, into his own. Epicurus, one of the ancient philosophers Stevens greatly admired, observed "that deeply ingrained habits of thought are not easily corrected, and . . . proposed various exercises to assist" in breaking their hold.[7]

Central in these exercises was the contemplation of nature and its processes: the world as meditation, in other words. It was not trivial that Stevens included an Eastern aesthetic in his project for "The Whole of Harmonium." He described that aesthetic as something "venerable, true, and quiet" (*L* 742). The North American continent— a region stretched physically between Europe and Asia and stretched in spirit between the aspiration of its first settlers, who thought themselves "citizens of heaven" about to found "a city upon a hill" and the actuality of history's most violent century—needs a new mythology. It was fitting, even therapeutic, that Stevens internalized lessons from Buddhism into his way of teaching. Clearly he was not alone in heeding its message: Schopenhauer, Peirce, and James, as noted earlier, as well as Ludwig Wittgenstein, Henri Bergson, and John Dewey were all plotting the meeting of East and West. On his deathbed Stevens asked his daughter to bring him one of his small statues of the Buddha so he could hold it in his hand.

Perhaps Stevens knew that early Buddhist psychology, in contrast to our later European and American forms, mapped and outlined 121 classes of consciousness and that of these, "sixty-three are accompanied by joy. The more man progresses, the more radiant and joyful will be his consciousness."[8] Spiraling up into ever widening circles in "the everlasting weather of our perceptions" as we participate in the "radiant and productive atmosphere" of Stevens's poems is a much-needed corrective—"modernity is so Chicagoan, so plain, so unmeditative"—to the idea of progress as it came to be understood in what Emerson called "this new yet unapproachable America we have found in the West."[9] Ascending through the mantic filigree of Stevens's lines one finds oneself more truly and more strange in the resting places of his stanzas, the rooms of his ideas, of his memory palace, where the places are held by the changing light of the planet moving through the "meadow of space."[10] Here one experiences "ecstatic identities / Between one's self and the weather."

ACKNOWLEDGMENTS

Robert D. Richardson, series editor for the University of Iowa Muse books, is in all ways the necessary angel of this volume. I also am immensely grateful to all those at the University of Iowa Press who worked to produce this beautiful edition. Elisabeth Chretien was the first to shepherd me and my pages through the process. Susan Hill Newton succeeded her with equal grace, engagement, and good humor. My dealings along the way with Catherine Cocks and Jim McCoy were most reassuring during a time of transition at the press. I also want to thank Judith Antonelli for scrupulous copyediting (increasingly rare these days) and Richard Hendel for the exquisite book design. (His idea for the interlineation of the two-part title is just brilliant!) Finally, Karen Copp's enthusiasm for my photo collage to use on the book's cover completed the round of pleasures I have enjoyed in composing and publishing this addition to the Muse series. My abiding gratitude to R. P. colors each of its pages—"The body dies; the body's beauty lives."

NOTES

CHAPTER 1: NOTATIONS OF THE WILD

1. William James, "What Psychical Research Has Accomplished," in *Writings, 1878–1899*, ed. Gerald E. Myers (New York: Library of America, 1992), 682: "if there is anything which human history demonstrates, it is the extreme slowness with which the ordinary academic and critical mind acknowledges facts to exist which present themselves as wild facts, with no stall or pigeonhole, or as facts which threaten to break up the accepted system."

2. Quoted in Joseph Leo Koerner, *Caspar David Friedrich and the Subject of Landscape* (London: Reaktion Books, 2009), 31. Notably including Stevens as part of his discussion, Koerner observes, "The early Romantics founded their metaphor of a world-book upon the traditional Christian conception of God as the author of two books: the Book of Scripture and the Book of Nature." This remark follows the quotation from Schlegel.

3. Ralph Waldo Emerson, *Essays and Lectures*, ed. Joel Porte (New York: Library of America, 1983), 761, 197, 92; hereafter *EL*.

4. Kiang Kang-Hu, *The Jade Mountain: A Chinese Anthology (Being Three Hundred Poems of the T'ang Dynasty, 618–906)*, trans. Witter Bynner (1929; repr., New York: Vintage, 1957), xxvi.

CHAPTER 2: ADEQUATE TO THIS GREAT HYMN

1. The transcription from this clipping and the details that follow concerning Stevens's reading of Psalms are drawn from my original research in the Wallace Stevens Collection at the Huntington Library. Joan Richardson, *Wallace Stevens: The Early Years, 1879–1923* (New York: Beech Tree Books, William

Morrow, 1986); and Joan Richardson, *Wallace Stevens: The Later Years, 1923–1955* (New York: Beech Tree Books, William Morrow, 1988).

2. Emerson, *EL*, 47.

3. Ibid.

4. For a full discussion of these phrases and concepts from Edwards, see Joan Richardson, *A Natural History of Pragmatism: The Fact of Feeling from Jonathan Edwards to Gertrude Stein* (Cambridge, UK: Cambridge University Press, 2007), 24–61.

5. Cleo McNelly Kearns, "Irigaray's *Between East and West*: Breath, Pranayama, and the Phenomenology of Prayer," in *The Phenomenology of Prayer*, ed. Bruce Ellis Benson and Norman Wirzba (New York: Fordham University Press, 2005), 112.

6. Emerson, *EL*, 126.

7. Ibid., 456.

8. Ibid., 23.

9. Ibid., 251: "Man is the broken giant, and, in all his weakness, both his body and his mind are invigorated by habits of conversation with nature."

10. William James, *Writings, 1902–1910*, ed. Bruce Kuklick (New York: Library of America, 1987), 36; emphasis in the original.

11. Ludwig Wittgenstein, *Philosophical Investigations*, trans. G. E. M. Anscombe (New York: Macmillian, 1968), sec. 115; emphasis in the original.

12. Cynthia Ozick, "'The Daemon Knows,' by Harold Bloom," *New York Times Book Review*, May 24, 2015.

CHAPTER 3: ECHOLOCATION

1. "All mean egotism vanishes" and "the currents of the Universal Being circulate through" belong to the famous "transparent eye-ball" passage in chapter 1 of *Nature* (1836); Emerson, *EL*, 10. The James quote is found in several of his works.

2. Samuel Taylor Coleridge, *Biographia Literaria: The Collected Works of Samuel Taylor Coleridge, Biographical Sketches of my Literary Life & Opinions*, vol. 7, ed. James Engell and

W. Jackson Bate (Princeton, NJ: Princeton University Press 1985), 295.

3. William James, "Telepathy," in *Johnson's Universal Cyclopedia: A New Edition Prepared by a Corps of Thirty-Six Editors, Assisted by Eminent European and American Specialists*, vol. 8 (New York: Appleton, 1899), 169.

4. Perry Miller, "Jonathan Edwards on 'The Sense of the Heart,'" *Harvard Theological Review* 41 (April 1948): 123–45.

5. "Critical opalescence" describes the extended intermediate state of a continuous phase transition between liquid and gas in which the density fluctuations become a size comparable to the wavelength of light, and so the light is scattered and causes a normally transparent liquid to "opalesce."

6. James, *Writings, 1902–1910*, 65, 72, 59; emphasis in the original.

CHAPTER 4: THE EXQUISITE ENVIRONMENT OF FACT

1. The title *Adagia* is borrowed from the Dutch humanist Erasmus's annotated collection of Greek and Latin proverbs, which he began compiling and commenting on early in his life and continued to add to until his death; the first edition, published in 1500, had around eight hundred entries, and the last had more than four thousand. Wikipedia has noted that many of the adages are commonplace in English and many European languages and that we owe our use of them to Erasmus. Although Stevens's collection is Spartan in comparison and each of his entries is original, the title reveals Erasmus to be "the hermit in [the] poet's metaphors."

2. The lovely phrase "century of intense thought" is taken from Carlo Rovelli, *Seven Brief Lessons on Physics*, trans. Simon Carnell and Erica Segre (New York: Riverhead Books, 2016), 14. This lucid little volume should be required reading for all.

3. Herwig Friedl, "Out of Bounds: American Visions of the Thinker and of Thinking," in *Intellectual Authority and Literary Culture in the US, 1790–1900*, ed. Gunter Leypoldt (Heidelberg: Universitatsverlag Winter, 2013), 211–12; emphasis in the original.

4. Charles Sanders Peirce, *The Collected Papers of Charles Sanders Peirce*, vol. 1, ed. Charles Hartshorne, Paul Weiss, and Arthur W. Burks (Cambridge, MA: Harvard University Press, 1932), par. 357. In opening *Nature* Emerson asked, "Why should not we also enjoy an original relation to the universe?" Emerson, *EL*, 7.

5. Alfred North Whitehead, *Science and the Modern World: Lowell Lectures, 1925* (New York: Free Press, 1953), 143–44, 147.

6. Ibid., 2.

7. Ibid., 3.

CHAPTER 5: THE SOUND OF WORDS

1. William James, *The Principles of Psychology* (1890; repr., Cambridge, MA: Harvard University Press, 1983), 63.

2. Richardson, *Natural History of Pragmatism*, 228–29.

3. Emerson, *EL*, 663.

4. Quoted in Susan Sontag, *On Photography* (New York: Penguin, 2008), 145.

5. Nicholas Myklebust, "'Bergamo on a Postcard'; or, A Critical History of Cognitive Poetics," *Wallace Stevens Journal* 39, no. 2 (Fall 2015): 149. Myklebust offers a brilliant reading of Stevens's "The Plot against the Giant" in which he observes, "The vehicle for speech and a metonym for poetry, sound is the most cognitively complex of the three sensory modalities"—the other two operating in the poem are smell and sight. Taste and touch are less complex than these other two, so I have generalized sound to be "the most cognitively complex."

6. Jonathan Edwards, "The Mind," in *The Works of Jonathan Edwards*, vol. 6, *Scientific and Philosophical Writings*, ed. Wallace E. Anderson (New Haven, CT: Yale University Press, 1980), 345.

7. Hans Blumenberg, *Paradigms for a Metaphorology* (Ithaca, NY: Cornell University Press, 2010), 63, 64.

8. Emerson, *EL*, xxx.

CHAPTER 6: MAN ON THE DUMP

1. Sontag, *On Photography*, 153; emphasis in the original.

2. Quoted in C. K. Ogden and I. A. Richards, "Appendix D: Some Moderns," in *The Meaning of Meaning: A Study of the Influence of Language upon Thought and of the Science of Symbolism* (1923; repr., New York: Harcourt Brace Jovanovich, 1946), 280–81.

3. Ibid., 279.

4. James, *Writings, 1902–1910*, 1150–51; emphasis in the original.

5. Mark J. Bruhn, "A Mirror on the Mind: Stevens, Chiasmus, and Autim Spectrum Disorder," *Wallace Stevens Journal* 39, no. 2 (Fall 2015): 185.

6. Ibid.

7. Ibid., 200.

8. Ibid.

9. Ibid., 197.

10. Ibid., 182; James, *Writings, 1902–1910*, 448–49.

11. In "The Transcendentalist," Emerson wrote, "I—this thought which is called I,—is the mould into which the world is poured like melted wax. This mould is invisible, but the world betrays the shape of the mould." Emerson, *EL*, 196.

12. James, *Principles of Psychology*, 246. The full sentence is "It is, in short, the re-instatement of the vague to its proper place in our mental life which I am so anxious to press on the attention."

13. James, *Writings, 1902–1910*, 863.

CHAPTER 7: DARKEN YOUR SPEECH

1. Alfred North Whitehead, *Adventures of Ideas* (1931; repr., New York: Free Press, 1961), 72.

2. Ralph Waldo Emerson, *Letters and Social Aims* (Boston: James R. Osgood, 1876), 11.

3. Edward Hirsch, *The Demon and the Angel: Searching for the Source of Artistic Inspiration* (New York: Harcourt Books, 2002), xi.

4. This and the earlier "All that has dark sounds" quotation are

from Federico García Lorca, "Theory and Play of the *Duende*," Poetry in Translation, http://www.poetryintranslation.com.

5. Kelefa Sanneh, "White Mischief: The Passions of Carl Van Vechten," *New Yorker*, February 17 and 24, 2014, 103. Sanneh noted that Van Vechten's best-selling book *Nigger Heaven* "helped draw attention to a movement: the Negro Renaissance, which came to be known, and celebrated, as the Harlem Renaissance" (100). Van Vechten enjoyed a forty-year friendship with Langston Hughes as well as friendships with Bessie Smith, Countee Cullen, and Nella Larsen—in fact, he was one of the earliest supporters of Larsen's work. Stevens described Van Vechten as *Harmonium*'s "*accoucheur*" in a note accompanying his gift to him of the volume (*L* 241).

6. Sanneh, "White Mischief," 106.

7. Ezra Pound, "Hugh Selwyn Mauberly (Life and Contacts)," in *Personae: The Shorter Poems of Ezra Pound* (New York: New Directions, 1926), 188.

8. Sontag, *On Photography*, 73.

9. "The thought of what America would be like" is from Ezra Pound, "Cantico del Sole," in *Personae*, 182; however, the context is quite different.

CHAPTER 8: PROPERTIES OF LIGHT

1. John Berger, *Understanding a Photograph* (New York: Penguin, 2013), 49, 58.

2. Ibid., 14.

3. Sontag, *On Photography*, 93; first emphasis added.

4. Berger, *Understanding a Photograph*, 59, 100.

5. Ibid., 100.

6. Sontag, *On Photography*, 95–96.

7. Quoted in ibid., 97.

8. Ibid., 115.

9. For a full discussion of Edwards's appropriation of Newton's description of the nature and behavior of light in his elucidation of grace, see Richardson, *Natural History of Pragmatism*, 24–61.

10. Sontag, *On Photography*, 118, 122.

1. A detailed analysis of this poem and how it serves as a guide to reading Stevens in general can be found in Richardson, *Natural History of Pragmatism*, 179–231.

2. Douglas Shadle, "Nothing Ordinary about It: The Mass Proper as Early Music Jigsaw Puzzle," *Journal of Music History Pedagogy* 3, no. 1 (2012): 4.

3. For a full account of this occasion, see Richardson, *Natural History of Pragmatism*, 208–16.

CHAPTER 10: PLANET ON THE TABLE

1. "Cosmic consciousness" is from James, *Writings, 1902–1910*, 359: "The prime characteristic of cosmic consciousness is a consciousness of the cosmos, that is, of the life and order of the universe. Along with the consciousness of the cosmos there occurs an intellectual enlightenment which alone would place the individual on a new plane of existence—would make him almost a member of a new species." James himself got the term from Richard Maurice Bucke's *Cosmic Consciousness: A Study in the Evolution of the Human Mind* (1901).

2. Rovelli, *Seven Brief Lessons*, 10.

3. Ludwig Wittgenstein, *Tractatus Logico-Philosophicus*, trans. C. K. Ogden (1921; repr., New York: Routledge, 2001), sec. 6.44.

4. Emerson, *EL*, 459.

5. John Banville, "'A Beautiful and Closely Woven Tapestry,'" *New York Review of Books*, November 5, 2015, 60.

6. Friedrich Nietzsche, *Twilight of the Idols*, trans. R. J. Hollingdale (New York: Penguin Classics, 1990), 48. The German: "*Ich fürchte, wir warden Gott nicht los, weil wir noch an die Grammatik glauben.*"

7. Emerson, *EL*, 463.

8. James, *Principles of Psychology*, 253–55; emphasis added.

9. Ibid., 254.

10. Emerson, *EL*, 409.

11. James, *Writings, 1902–1910*, 385.

12. The figure of the "axis of vision" is also from *Nature*: "The

ruin or the blank, that we see when we look at nature, is in our own eye. The axis of vision is not coincident with the axis of things, and so they appear not transparent but opake," Emerson, *EL*, 47. "This planet . . . most wonderful" is from Charles Darwin, *On the Origin of Species: A Facsimile of the First Edition*, ed. Ernst Mayr (Cambridge, MA: Harvard University Press, 2001), 490.

CHAPTER 11: IT CAN NEVER BE SATISFIED,
THE MIND, NEVER

1. John Tyndall, "The Scientific Use of Imagination," *Fragments of Science*, vol. 2 (London: Longmans, Green, 1892; London: Gregg International, 1970), 104.

2. James, *Principles of Psychology*, 220.

3. Henry James, "John Tyndall," in Henry James, *Literary Criticism: Essays on Literature: American Writers, English Writers*, ed. Leon Edel (New York: Library of America, 1984), 1357.

4. Emerson, *EL*, 669.

5. Timothy D. Wilson, *Strangers to Ourselves: Discovering the Adaptive Unconscious* (Cambridge, MA: Harvard University Press, 2002), 24.

6. James, *Principles of Psychology*, 236–39; emphasis in the original.

7. Ibid., 235.

8. Ibid.

9. Blumenberg, *Paradigms*, 7; emphasis in the original. For a full discussion, see Hans Blumenberg, "Light as a Metaphor of Truth," trans. Joel Anderson, in *Modernity and the Hegemony of Vision*, ed. David Levin (Berkeley: University of California Press, 1993), 30–62.

10. J. A. Baker, quoted in John Gray, *The Silence of the Animals: On Progress and Other Modern Myths* (New York: Farrar, Straus and Giroux, 2014), 156.

1. Swami Vivekananda, *Vedanta Philosophy: Lectures on Jnana Yoga* (New York: Vedanta Society, 1902; London: Forgotten Books, 2012), 211.

2. Nolan Pliny Jacobson, *The Heart of Buddhist Philosophy* (Carbondale: Southern Illinois University Press, 2010), 71–72.

3. Ibid., 114.

4. Berger, *Understanding a Photograph*, 77–78.

CHAPTER 13: THE IMPERFECT IS OUR PARADISE

1. Emerson, *EL*, 46.

2. Herwig Friedl, "Thinking in Search of a Language: Pragmatism and the Muted Middle Voice," *American Studies* 47, no. 4 (2002): 480, 482.

3. Louis Martz, "Wallace Stevens: The World as Meditation," *Yale Review* 47 (1958): 517–36; Frank Kermode, quoted in Jeannine Johnson, *Why Write Poetry: Modern Poets Defending Their Art* (Madison, NJ: Fairleigh Dickinson University Press, 2007), 110.

4. The phrase "an interval in the life of the mind" is from the discussion of Stevens's "A Dish of Peaches in Russia" in Gray, *Silence of the Animals*, 207.

5. For an extended and excellent analysis of neoliberalism and its current consequences, see George Monbiot, "Neoliberalism—the Ideology at the Root of All Our Problems," *Guardian*, April 15, 2016, http://gu.com/p/4tbfb?CMP=Share_iOSApp_Other. I have quoted from this pertinent paragraph: "So pervasive has neoliberalism become that we seldom even recognize it as an ideology. We appear to accept the proposition that this utopian, millenarian faith describes a neutral force; a kind of biological law, like Darwin's theory of evolution. But the philosophy arose as a conscious attempt to reshape human life and shift the locus of power." I am grateful to my dear friend, the poet Ann Lauterbach, for alerting me to this piece.

6. John Gray, *Straw Dogs: Thoughts on Humans and Other Animals* (New York: Farrar, Straus and Giroux, 2007), 41.

7. Quoted in Andrew Levy, "The Particulars of Subtle Fitness

and Its Uses for Life," in *Supple Science: A Robert Kocik Primer*, ed. Michael Cross and Thom Donovan (Oakland, CA: ON Contemporary Practice, 2014), 14.

8. Lama Anagarika Govinda, quoted in Jacobson, *Buddhism and the Contemporary World*, 68.

9. Emerson, *EL*, 485.

10. Ibid., 456.

INDEX

.